Also by William B. Mead

Even the Browns: The Zany, True Story of Baseball in the Early Forties

With Mike Feinsilber:
American Averages: Amazing Facts of Everyday Life

THE OFFICIAL
New York Yankees Hater's
HANDBOOK

WILLIAM B. MEAD

A PERIGEE BOOK

Perigee Books
are published by
G. P. Putnam's Sons
200 Madison Avenue
New York, New York 10016

Library of Congress Cataloging in Publication Data

Mead, William B.
The official New York Yankees hater's handbook.

"A Perigee book."
1. New York Yankees (Baseball team) — History —
Anecdotes, facetiae, satire, etc. I. Title.
GV875.N4M383   1983   796.357'64'097471   82-18966
ISBN 0-399-50723-X

First Perigee printing, 1983.
Printed in the United States of America

1   2   3   4   5   6   7   8   9

Designed by Elizabeth Woll

To Ma, who likes to share a good laugh

Acknowledgments

My son, Chris, shared the research. We chuckled together as we culled facts and anecdotes from Jim Bouton's *Ball Four*; Peter Golenbock's *Dynasty*, *Bronx Zoo* (with Sparky Lyle) and *Number One* (with Billy Martin); Bill Veeck's *Veeck as in Wreck* and *Hustler's Handbook*; Donald Honig's *Baseball When the Grass Was Real*, *Baseball Between the Lines*, and *The October Heroes*; Maury Allen's *Where Have You Gone, Joe DiMaggio?*; Nathan Salant's *This Date in New York Yankees History*; Robert Creamer's *Babe: The Legend Comes to Life*; numerous other books, and countless articles from *The Sporting News*, *Sports Illustrated*, *Sport*, *Esquire*, the *New York Times*, the *Washington Post* and other publications.

My brother, Alden, researched and wrote the epilogue, and joined me in Florida for interviews with the players, past and present, who are quoted. All these men were patient, thoughtful and helpful, and I thank them. The only team that wouldn't cooperate was the New York Yankees. "We get enough of that stuff from the writers we *have* to help," a weary publicist said.

Bob Broeg of the *St. Louis Post-Dispatch* contributed several funny anecdotes. Paul Heacock supervised much of the photography. Cliff Kachline, historian at the National Baseball Hall of Fame; Bob Davids, president of the Society for American Baseball Research; Dave Kelly of the Library of Congress, and Phil Wood were extremely helpful. Others helped, too, and I apologize for not naming them all. Bows also to Henry Wadsworth Longfellow, Robert Service, Ernest L. Thayer, and Sigmond Romberg who wrote the song "Stout-Hearted Men."

Purists contend that an author should proclaim his leanings up front. Fair enough. I love the St. Louis Cardinals and the Baltimore Orioles. On a given day against the Yankees, I can love any team.

—WILLIAM B. MEAD

CONTENTS

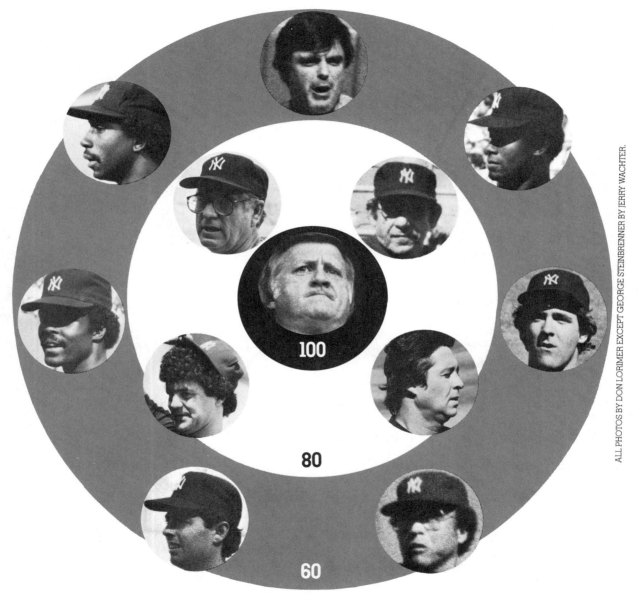

100

80

60

A Yankee Hater's Dartboard, Circa 1982.

INTRODUCTION

WE hate the New York Yankees for many reasons.

They're spoiled rotten.

They think they're such Hot Stuff.

Their owner is obnoxious.

They pout, sulk and whine, no matter how much they're paid and pampered.

Their fans are gross and crude.

I could go on, and I will. So could you. That's what this book is about. Most all good Americans hate the Yankees. It is a value we cherish and pass along to our children, like decency and democracy and the importance of a good breakfast. Along with the Pledge of Allegiance, hatred of the Yankees should be part of the naturalization test for new U.S. citizens. If it were, everybody would pass.

Yankee propaganda buffets and surrounds us, yet the truth shines through. Russian television carries yet another Andropov speech on Saturday afternoon; NBC carries yet another Yankee game. Tass boasts proudly of Russian armor; American newspapers spew nonsense about the "dreaded pinstripes."

With forked tongue, Yankee propagandists tell innocent young Americans that today's loathsome Yankees are unlike their noble predecessors. This is a lie. Fathers and mothers, grandfathers and grandmothers, great-grandfathers and great-grandmothers fondly recall the Yankee-hatred of their own youth and the ignoble athletes who spawned it. History tells us that most great evils have been stamped out — Attila, Hitler, Prohibition, the plague, Corfam shoes — yet the Yankees crawl on.

Yankee fans tell us that we hate the Yankees because they win. Oh yeah? Did anyone hate them less in 1982, when they laid eggs all season and finished one game out of last place? Did Americans cuddle the rich, whimpering Yankees to their breasts? No! Yankee hatred — a happy, exultant hatred — bloomed and flourished as never before. Our land was blessed; even the weather that summer was mild and bright and glorious. Fans booed and hooted and jeered the Yankees, and their happy cries rose to heaven in a glorious HALLELUJAH! Win or lose, the Yankees are hateful.

Their wealth is hateful. The whole team was bought, even the bad players, and so were Yankee teams of the past.

Their arrogance is hateful. Know whose plaque is out behind centerfield at Yankee Stadium, along with Ruth, Gehrig and DiMaggio? Pope Paul VI! Since when was he a Yankee? For God's sake, get him out of there! Free the Pope!

But let's waste no time on anguish. Yankee haters get enough of that. This book is dedicated to Yankee failures and humiliations. Moments when the forces of Right and Goodness prevailed. Petty Yankee embarrassments, delicious Yankee catastrophes.

Many of the stories in this book are personal, recounted by men who lived them. Grover Cleveland Alexander is dead, but Les Bell, the old Cardinal third baseman, recalls Alexander's dramatic strikeout of Tony Lazzeri in the 1926 World Series. Pee Wee Reese and Roy Campanella tell of the great catch by Sandy Amoros that won the 1955 World Series for the Brooklyn Dodgers. Steve Garvey savors the Los Angeles Dodgers' comeback in the 1981 World Series.

Other triumphs are recalled by Hall of Famers Joe Cronin, Al Lopez, Stan Musial and Sandy Koufax; by Walt Alston, Lew Burdette, Jim Kaat, Tom Seaver, Jim Palmer, Sparky Anderson, Johnny Bench, Tony Perez, and others.

This book punctures many myths and deflates many egos. It pays no homage to Yankee scripture, past or present. It presents Yankee failures with hosannas, Yankee misfortunes with prayers of thanks.

All this is written as good, clean fun. There is no malice intended. I boo the Yankees, but I don't throw things at them, and I don't think anyone should. The stories, facts and anecdotes in this book are true, to the best of my knowledge. For any errors, I apologize in advance — even to a Yankee.

Yankee haters, arise!

CHAPTER ONE

The Roots and Traditions of Yankee-Hating

THE first Yankee haters were New Yorkers.

They were fans of the New York Giants, who preceded the Yankees in town and earned the devotion of local baseball fans. Giant fans had reason to look down on the rest of baseball, and they viewed the Yankees with contempt. Under Manager John McGraw, the Giants won six pennants while the Yankees were still floundering after their first.

When the Yankees finally bought their first pennant, in 1921, they found themselves facing the lordly Giants in the World Series. The Giants won that Series, five games to three. The Giants and Yankees won pennants again the next season, and the Giants swept that World Series, four games to none.

By that time, hatred of the Yankees was fanning across America like a sweet spring breeze, nowhere more than in Boston, where the Red Sox owner, Harry Frazee, had raped a championship team, position by position, in exchange for Yankee gold. When the Yankees won their first world championship in 1923, their roster listed eleven former Red Sox stars, including Babe Ruth. The Red Sox, champions as recently as 1918, had embarked on a miserable nine-season slide in which they would finish last every year but one. "When they talk about the Yankee dynasty," recalled Ernie Shore, one of many pitchers sold from Boston to New York, "I always say it was really a Red Sox dynasty, in a Yankee uniform."

Walter Catlett, the late character actor, once told of an evening in Boston with the expansive Frazee and two young ladies. "We had a couple of cupcakes, and Harry wanted to impress them," Catlett recalled. "So he told the cabdriver to take us to Fenway Park."

Once there, Frazee talked proudly of his team. He even got out of the cab to gesture grandly at his stadium. The cabdriver overheard, and got out with him. "Excuse me, sir. Do you own the Red Sox?"

"That's right, my good man."

"Then you're the man who sold Babe Ruth to the Yankees?"

Frazee grunted an acknowledgment, whereupon the cabbie decked him with a hard right. Frazee landed on the pavement, a mild enough punishment for his sins. His dignity was lost along with his aspirations concerning the cupcakes.

Boston fans were not the only ones with reason to hate the Yankees. In 1922 the St. Louis Browns, of all people, fought the Yankees tooth and nail all season. In what was already becoming a tradition, the Yankees tipped the pennant race in their own favor on July 23 by acquiring Joe Dugan, a star third baseman, from — guess who — the Red Sox.

St. Louis fans were incensed. The Chamber of Commerce adopted a resolution denouncing the Yankees for lack of sportsmanship. When the Yankees came to St. Louis for a decisive series in mid-September, Brownie fans were waiting. Sportsman's Park was sold out and fans stood behind ropes in the outfield.

In the first game, with Brownies on base, a fly ball was lofted to center field. Whitey Witt, the Yankee outfielder, chased it, raised his glove, and — CONK — fell to the ground, bleeding and unconscious. The missile was a pop bottle, which caught Witt square on the forehead. Witnesses swore that the culprit, or hero, was an eleven-year-old boy. Had he been identified, he might now be enshrined with Stan Musial and Bob Gibson in the St. Louis Sports Hall of Fame.

Bob Meusel, the Yankee left fielder, looked into the crowd, perhaps expecting sympathy for his fallen teammate. "We'll get you too, Meusel!" a fan called. But they didn't, and the Yankees went on to win that game and the pennant. The Browns did not gain revenge until they won their only pennant twenty-two years later.

As America has grown and prospered, expressions of hatred toward the Yankees have flared in every city, in every era. Time and Yankee propaganda have had a softening effect on history, leaving the impression that Americans used to love the Yankees and root them on. Not so; fans have always turned out to root against the Yankees, not for them. Some fans have braved great personal risk, like the hero in Washington, D.C. who decided that *someone* had to stop Joe DiMaggio's hitting streak in 1941. This selfless man vaulted onto the field between games of a doubleheader in old Griffith Stadium and made off with DiMaggio's favorite bat. It didn't work — Senator pitchers were not the kind to stop a hitting streak, no matter the bat or batter — but that fan's heroism should not go unrecorded.

Some Yankee-hating demonstrations have been tame, like the booing heaped on DiMaggio at every stop, including New York, after he held out in 1938 for $40,000, more than Lou Gehrig was making. The IYC (Immortal Yankee Clipper) finally signed for $25,000, but the fans were not forgiving.

After the Yankees beat the White Sox 18 to 2 in

12

Chicago one June day in 1953, a Chicago waiter refused to serve Casey Stengel, and a cabdriver threatened a kamikaze crash knowing he would die, but so would the creatures who had crawled into his cab — Yankees Yogi Berra, Joe Collins and Charlie Silvera.

During spring training of 1963, Yankee relief pitcher Marshall (Sheriff) Bridges made friendly overtures to a pretty young thing at the Fort Lauderdale Elks Lodge. She pulled a pistol and shot the surprised reliever in the left leg.

That's overdoing it, but in their fantasies fans and players have done worse. Davey Lopes, then the Dodger second baseman, suggested after the 1978 World Series that Yankee Stadium be bombed. Three years later, Lopes and his Dodger teammates gained revenge more peacefully, bombing the Yankees in the 1981 World Series.

These days, hatred, like other things, is better organized. Pete Franklin, a popular sports talk-show host on radio station WWWE in Cleveland, staged his first "Hate the Yankees Hanky Night" on September 5, 1977. Inspired by 28,184 fans waving hankies inscribed "I Hate the Yankees," the Indians broke an eighteen-game losing streak against New York with a 4 to 3, 5 to 4 sweep. Franklin and the Indians have repeated this healthy and cheerful promotion every year, although the Indian brass has progressively sissified the affair by insisting that it be renamed first "Beat the Yankees Hanky Night" and, by 1982, simply "Hanky Night." Franklin has no such qualms; he calls himself America's biggest Yankee hater, a bold claim considering the nationwide competition. When Yankee fans call in to his show, Franklin asks them where they are from. If

they are from New York, he forgives them. If not, he berates them.

The Baltimore Orioles have been the Yankees' most consistent rivals in recent years. During a dull game between the Orioles and Toronto several years ago, Gordon Beard of the Associated Press suggested a test for the apathetic Baltimore fans. Reggie Jackson was then with the Yankees, and Rex Barney, a former Dodger pitcher who works as the Orioles' public address announcer, fabricated this message:

"Will the owner of the automobile bearing the license plate, 'New York R-E-G 44...' "

Barney didn't get to finish his announcement. He didn't even get to the R-E-G 44. "As soon as he said 'New York,' the entire crowd got up and booed," recalls an Oriole official. The Orioles have repeated this little joke several times, always with the same results. "We don't need to do it when the Yankees are here, because the fans have something right in front of them that they can boo," the official explains.

Yankee Hating is a helpless condition. Bob Brown, the veteran public relations director of the Orioles, has sometimes struggled against it on occasions when a Yankee victory would benefit Baltimore. "Even if it would be better for the Yankees to win that game," Brown says, "I can't root for them."

Many veteran players feel the same way. Charlie Gehringer, a Hall of Fame second baseman who helped the Detroit Tigers win pennants in 1934, 1935 and 1940, is cheerfully incredulous when approached on the subject. "Who do I root for? You mean who do I root *against*. The Yankees!" Somewhat sheepishly, Gehringer confess-

Charlie Gehringer: He still roots against the Yankees. DETROIT TIGERS

es allegiance to the American League; after all, he played nineteen seasons for Detroit. "When the Yankees are playing in a World Series, I kind of pull for them," he says. "But not too hard."

Most present-day players deny any dislike of the Yankees, partly to avoid antagonizing a potential employer. "Who knows what will happen? I might end up there some day," says Jerry Reuss, the Dodger lefthander. "I don't hate the bleeping Yankees." He smiles. "But I don't love 'em."

Players are less diplomatic about the fans at

Yankee Stadium, who are widely renowned for their boorish vulgarity. Listen to Ken Singleton, the Orioles' veteran slugger: "Yankee fans have a way of making you play harder, because they really get on the opposition. They're boisterous, and they've been known to shower the opposition — literally. You go up there and you want to show these people that you deserve to be recognized as a human being, let alone as a ballplayer."

Sometimes, however, even the Yankee fans must feel that they are not recognized as human beings. On October 2, 1982, the Yankees staged what they called "Fan Appreciation Day" — and celebrated it, according to witnesses quoted in the New York *Daily News*, by beating up two of their own fans. The fans, Dennis Denbeck and Joe Turnbull, both 32, committed the sin of putting brown paper bags over their heads in comic protest of the Yankees' delightfully dismal season. Yankee security guards told them to leave and, when they protested, the guards swung at them, called in reinforcements, and pummelled poor Denbeck and Turnbull into a true appreciation of the Yankees' style and character.

Perhaps the guards' actions were only retribution; Yankee fans had had their turn earlier in the season, on the glorious night of April 27, 1982, when Reggie Jackson returned to Yankee Stadium for the first time in the uniform of the California Angels. Jackson had singled and scored a run, then, in a steady drizzle verging on rain, hit a monstrous home run into what had once been "his" right field seats as the Angels thumped the Yankees. Jackson's appearance coincided with the first stop of the '82 managerial merry-go-round — Bob Lemon fired for the second time, Gene Michael hired for the second

14

Ken Singleton's home-run trot. JERRY WACHTER: BALTIMORE ORIOLES

time — and the fans decided that even for the Yankees, all this was too much. With George Steinbrenner huddled miserably in a box seat, thirty-five thousand of his own fans rose and, as Jackson completed his home run trot, broke into a spontaneous and sustained two-word chant. "Steinbrenner sucks," the fans said. "Steinbrenner sucks; Steinbrenner sucks; Steinbrenner sucks!"

Reggie's angelic homer sent a cascade of epithets in Steinbrenner's direction. He's almost atoned for having been a Yankee. CALIFORNIA ANGELS

15

STEINBRENNER SUCKS!

The Yankee team had fallen deep
When George awoke it from its sleep
He raised the team through strength of dollar
And yet he heard the grandstand holler
      Steinbrenner sucks!

"Oh, stay in shipping," the young maid said,
"And let me soothe your blow-dried head."
He turned away and said goodbye
And went to face that raucous cry
      Steinbrenner sucks!

He courted Catfish from his lair
And made the players cut their hair
His voice rang out in stern demand
And fans roared back throughout the land
      Steinbrenner sucks!

With treasure from his father's chest
He purchased Reggie, Goose, the rest
The pennants flew in proud display
And still the fans would only say
      Steinbrenner sucks!

He hired Bold Billy, the Stick and Lem
And then twice-fired the three of them
He praised New York, he loved the town
And still that clarion voice rolled down
      Steinbrenner sucks!

He sat one night, his face distraught
Among the fans whose love he sought
"I'm one of you!" his damp eyes pled
The fans stood up and loudly said
      Steinbrenner sucks!

He dreamed of Yankees stealing bases
Banished Reggie, hired new faces
He filled the team with Reds and Twins
Said the fans, their bellies full of him
      Steinbrenner sucks!

In Yankee stadium, cold and still
He stood alone in winter's chill
His shoes were shined, his tie was neat
Yet a cry rolled out from the empty seats
      Steinbrenner sucks!

JERRY WACHTER

CHAPTER TWO

A QUIZ FOR YANKEE HATERS

A HALF-DOZEN correct answers qualifies you as a Good American. Get twenty right and you should be elected to high public office. Anyone who gets twenty-five is a saint. If the answers make you unhappy, you are a Yankee fan. Go away.

Answers start on page 20.

1. Not counting 1982, what American League team has gone the longest without a losing season?

2. Why did George Steinbrenner ask his biographer, Dick Schaap, to drop the project?

3. What did Babe Ruth, Roger Maris and Reggie Jackson have in common?

4. Whom did the Yankees virtually bribe to play for them in 1982?

5. Name the Yankee managers, batting coaches, and pitching coaches of 1982. Five names earns you a point; anyone batting twelve for twelve has passed the quiz.

6. Who is Bob Sykes, and why does he epitomize George Steinbrenner's trading acumen?

7. Who was the last Yankee to make a run at a .400 batting average? Dave Winfield? Mickey Mantle? Joe DiMaggio? Some other turkey?

8. Against what team did Babe Ruth hit his first major league home run? His first record-setting home run?

9. What Yankee outfielder made four errors in one day?

10. What record did Mickey Mantle tie during the 1953 World Series?

11. How did the Yankees celebrate Billy Martin's twenty-ninth birthday?

12. Don Larsen pitched a perfect game in the fifth game of the 1956 World Series. What other pitching mark did he set in that series?

13. What did catcher Yogi Berra say to Larsen after the perfect game?

14. How did Larsen's wife celebrate his perfect game?

15. What was the Yankees' contribution to New York during the city's fiscal crisis of the 1970s?

16. How did Reggie Jackson and Graig Nettles celebrate the Yankees' clinching of the 1981 pennant?

17. How close were Babe Ruth and Lou Gehrig, and what sentiment did Ruth's daughter express about Gehrig and his family?

18. What do Yankee players of the '80s mean when they talk of the "Dark Cloud"?

19. In the only beanball death in baseball history, Yankee pitcher Carl Mays killed

Ray Chapman of the Cleveland Indians on August 16, 1920. How did Mays react to the tragedy? How did the Indians react?

20. For years Joe DiMaggio had flowers placed upon the grave of Marilyn Monroe, and the depth of their love is often commented upon. How long were they together?

21. Who was the Baby Ruth candy bar named after?

22. What Yankee smashed the most controversial hits during the 1981 World Series?

23. What personal sacrifice earned Yankee shortstop Tony Kubek a full page in *Sports Illustrated*?

24. What did Mickey Mantle and Billy Martin do together at night as newlyweds?

25. How did the Yankees reward the shapely blonde in Chicago who displayed her admiration on the team bus three straight days in 1979?

26. After he retired as a player, Joe DiMaggio did short television shows before and after Yankee games. One day he threatened not to do a show because the cue card with his opening line was missing. What was this difficult opening line?

27. What expensive crop grew on the Kentucky farm of Yankee pitcher Don Gullett?

28. Whom did the Yankees select to replace Bucky Harris as manager after the 1948 season?

29. Who was Delores Dixon?

30. What national award has George Steinbrenner won twice in recognition of his achievements as Yankee owner?

31. What military rank was achieved by Ralph Houk, former Yankee manager?

32. What is Goose Gossage's record in All-Star games?

33. Of all the sappy books about the Yankees, which is the sappiest?

34. How many World Series have the Yankees won in the last twenty years? Fourteen? Nine? Five? Two?

35. What major league team has won the most games in history through 1982?

Answers for Yankee Haters

1. The Boston Red Sox, who have not had a losing season since 1966. The Baltimore Orioles had their most recent losing season in 1967. The Yankees played below .500 as recently as 1973, not to mention their dismal record in 1982.

2. Steinbrenner said he wanted to write his own autobiography as an inspiration to American youth. No kidding.

3. All three crudely displayed their wealth. Ruth made several times as much salary as any other player and would wave his paycheck in the clubhouse and taunt his teammates about their meagre pay. Jackson liked to pull rolls of hundred-dollar bills and count them in public. Maris had a habit of exchanging insults with fans; to prove his superiority, he would say, "Oh yeah? How much money are *you* making?" This amused Maris's teammates, and when the outfielder got into arguments other Yankees gave him this taunting advice: "Hit him with your wallet!"

4. The Yankees paid John Mayberry $200,000 to accept a trade from Toronto to the hardship post of Yankee Stadium. Mayberry was past his prime, and spent most of the season on the Yankee bench.

5. The 1982 managers were Bob Lemon (won six, lost eight); Gene Michael (won forty-four, lost forty-two) and Clyde King (won twenty-nine, lost thirty-three). The batting coaches were Mickey Vernon, Joe Pepitone, Yogi Berra and Lou Piniella. The pitching coaches were Jeff Torborg, Jerry Walker, Stan Williams, Clyde King and Sammy Ellis.

6. Sykes is a pitcher whom the Yankees acquired from the Cardinals before the 1982 season in exchange for Willie McGee, a rookie outfielder. Sykes was a proven failure, having flunked five trials with the Tigers and Cardinals. He lived up to his promise, failing to make the weak Yankee pitching staff. McGee won a starting job with the Cardinals, led the National League in batting much of the 1982 season, and helped St. Louis to the championship. Way to pick 'em, George!

7. A turkey named Ron Blomberg, who was hitting .408 in early July of 1973. His career quickly tailed off, and he is best remembered as a trencherman who could down a 5-pound roast.

8. As a rookie with the Boston Red Sox, Ruth hit his first home run against Jack Warhop of the Yankees on May 6, 1915. On September 24, 1919, Ruth — still with Boston — hit his twenty-eighth home run of the season, breaking a record set in 1884. The Yankees were the opposing team.

9. Joe DiMaggio, on Memorial Day, 1941, during his fifty-six-game hitting streak.

10. Mantle struck out five straight times, four of them against Dodger pitcher Carl Erskine.

11. By banishing him to the Kansas City Athletics. Martin, Hank Bauer, Mickey Mantle, Whitey Ford, Yogi Berra and Johnny Kucks, all Yankee teammates, celebrated Martin's birthday with a party at the Copacabana nightclub in New York on May 16, 1957. A fight broke out, and a fellow named Edward Jones was knocked cold in the men's room. George Weiss, the Yankee general manager, blamed Martin, and traded him to Kansas City.

12. Larsen started the second game, in which the Yankees got bombed, 13 to 8 — the most runs ever yielded by the Yankees in a World Series game.

13. "Great game, Don."

14. She filed for divorce that very day.

15. They conned the impoverished city into refurbishing Yankee Stadium at a cost of more than $100 million.

16. They got into a boorish fight at a team party.

17. They were friends until Gehrig rejected Ruth's suggestion in 1929 that the two of them hold out together for higher salaries. After that, Ruth was contemptuous of Gehrig, and for some time the two men avoided each other. "The Ruths don't speak to the Gehrigs," said Julia Ruth, eighteen.

18. Bobby Murcer earned that nickname for his dour complaints about being benched.

19. Mays didn't seem to be bothered. Two days after Chapman was buried, Mays pitched again, and threw a shutout. Several teams threatened to strike if Mays continued pitching, but no action was taken. The Indians rose up and won the pennant.

20. She left DiMaggio after nine months, complaining that all he wanted to do was watch television.

21. President Grover Cleveland's daughter, Ruth. A bar called Babe Ruth's Home Run Candy was later introduced, but it was ruled in violation of the Baby Ruth copyright, and was removed from the market. However, Ruth did have a cigar named in his honor.

22. George Steinbrenner, who claimed that he beat up two nasty Dodger fans in a hotel elevator. The victims of Steinbrenner's blows vanished. Cynics have suggested that he punched the elevator wall.

23. Kubek sacrificed his brush cut and let his hair grow in exchange for $3,000 from Vitalis, which ran a full-page ad saying: "Tony Kubek knows

Oiled his hair for cash.

greasy creams and oils plaster down his hair, pile up on his comb. But Vitalis keeps his hair neat all day *without grease...*"

24. The Mantles and Martins lived in adjoining apartments, and the two young grooms occasionally sneaked to each other's bedroom window to watch the sexual action.

25. They autographed her bare posterior.

26. "Hi. I'm Joe DiMaggio. Welcome to *The Joe DiMaggio Show.*"

27. Marijuana, although Gullett didn't know it.

28. Billy Meyer, manager of the Pittsburgh Pirates. Only when Meyer declined did the Yankees hire Casey Stengel.

29. A woman from Long Island who filed a $50,000 paternity suit against Babe Ruth in 1925. The charge was dropped.

30. In 1980 and again in 1982, Steinbrenner won *TV Guide*'s "Mr. Nice Guy Award," which is presented annually to the sports figure who has best displayed "special boorish actions."

31. Houk, nicknamed "The Major," was an Army captain.

32. In three All-Star games through 1981, Gossage was rocked for an earned run average of 21.00. He had one loss and no wins.

33. The competition is tough. We'll allow one point if you picked any of these: *Where Have You Gone, Joe DiMaggio?*, by Maury Allen; *My Luke and I*, by Eleanor Gehrig and Joseph Durso; *The Babe Ruth Story*, ghosted by Bob Considine; *The Reggie Jackson Scrapbook*. Three points if you picked *And on the Eighth Day God Created the Yankees*, a dreadful and blasphemous work by one Vincent Bove, a sycophantic monk who got various Yankee players to write little homilies saying that all they care about is God, not money.

34. Two (1977 and 1978), and that's two too many.

35. The Chicago Cubs have won 8,060 games since their founding in 1876. The Yankees are more than 1,000 wins behind, with 7,028. Sure, the Cubs had a 27-year head start, but shouldn't they get credit for foresight?

CHAPTER THREE

HALL OF FAME

The All-Time Best Yankee Killers

FIRST BASE: Bill Terry. The last National Leaguer to bat .400, this New York Giant star of the '20s and '30s was so good that he kept Lou Gehrig from hogging all the first-base honors of his era. The ultimate squelch occurred June 3, 1932, when Gehrig hit four consecutive home runs in one game — and yet failed to lead the New York sports pages. The Gehrig story was trumped by the resignation of John McGraw, who had managed the Giants since 1902. Appropriately, Terry was named to succeed McGraw. The next season, Terry managed the Giants to the pennant, while the Yankees slipped to second place.

SECOND BASE: Rod (Hot Rod) Kanehl. This symbol of the New York Mets' inept charm cavorted at second base for three seasons, in all of which the Mets finished last and the Yankees first. By 1964, Kanehl's final season, the Mets were outdrawing the Yankees, and the Yankees were poised for their glorious plunge to eleven years of obscurity.

SHORTSTOP: Joe Hardy, a.k.a. Joe Boyd. This dashing young star from Hannibal, Missouri,

Joe Namath as Joe Hardy in a 1981 production of Damn Yankees, *in which Hardy sells his soul to the devil in exchange for one glorious season of stardom in which the Washington Senators beat the Yankees for the pennant.* MARTHA SWOPE, COURTESY OF BOB ULLMAN, PLAYWRIGHTS HORIZONS

Casey Stengel, when he was a good guy, scoring on his home run that beat the Yankees in the third game of the 1923 World Series. NATIONAL BASEBALL HALL OF FAME

propelled the Washington Senators to a pennant victory over the Yankees that is still enjoyed by thousands of Americans every year. Hardy was the hero of Douglass Wallop's hilarious novel, *The Year the Yankees Lost the Pennant*, which was made into the hit musical *Damn Yankees*. Boyd, a middle-aged Washington real estate agent, sells his soul to the Devil in exchange for a new identity as Hardy, the greatest baseball player in history. By happy coincidence, Wallop's book was published in 1954, a year the Yankees lost the pennant. ("Ya Gotta Have Heart!")

THIRD BASE: Ken Keltner. The Cleveland Indians' star made two outstanding plays on July 17, 1941, to stop Joe DiMaggio's hitting streak at fifty-six games.

OUTFIELD: Casey Stengel. Playing for the New York Giants, Stengel won two games of the 1923 World Series with home runs and gave the Yankee bench the finger as he rounded the bases.

OUTFIELD: Enos Slaughter. The heroic Cardinal star helped beat the Yankees in the 1942 World Series. When Slaughter was traded to the Yankees twelve years later, he openly wept at the awful news.

OUTFIELD: Pedro Guerrero. This lesser-known member of the 1981 Dodgers hit two homers and drove in seven runs to pace Los Angeles to its World Series victory over the Yankees. Guerrero hit one of the two homers that won the fifth Series game, 2 to 1. In the sixth and final game, he drove in five runs as the Dodgers won, 9 to 2.

CATCHER: Clint (Scrap Iron) Courtney. They don't come any tougher than Courtney, who

Pedro Guerrero, hero of the 1981 World Series. LOS ANGELES DODGERS

Scrap Iron Courtney, who took on the whole Yankee team. GEORGE BRACE

snarled at the pinstripes even as a member of the St. Louis Browns. After a Yankee runner bowled him over at the plate in a close game in 1953, Courtney came to bat, singled and barreled into second base, spikes high. He cut shortstop Phil Rizzuto and went down gamely fighting as four Yankees piled on him, fists swinging.

RIGHTHANDED PITCHER: Jackie Mitchell. A *woman* pitching against the Yanks? You bet, and she struck out Ruth and Gehrig on six pitches in an exhibition game April 1, 1931, at Chattanooga, Tennessee.

Jackie Mitchell: Ruth and Gehrig were no match for her strong right arm. She's shown here after throwing out the first ball of the 1981 season for the Chattanooga Lookouts, who invited her back to commemorate the 50th anniversary of her historic feat. PHILLIP SCHMIDT, CHATTANOOGA TIMES

Hubert (Shucks) Pruett of the St. Louis Browns,
who struck out Babe Ruth ten of the first eleven times
he faced him.

LEFTHANDED PITCHER: Hubert (Shucks) Pruett. He weighed only 135 pounds and played baseball only to pay his way through medical school, but this St. Louis Brown southpaw struck out Babe Ruth ten of the first eleven times he faced him. By the time Ruth had batted against Pruett seventeen times, he had one walk, one home run, and fifteen strikeouts.

PINCHHITTER: Cookie Lavagetto. With two outs in the ninth inning of the fourth World Series game of 1947, Lavagetto spoiled Yankee Bill Bevens's no-hitter with a double that won the game for Brooklyn, 3 to 2.

UMPIRE: Bill Dinneen. As a Red Sox pitcher, Dinneen won the first game ever between the Red Sox and Yankees and also beat the Yankees on the final day of the 1904 season to win the pennant for Boston. As an umpire in 1922, he threw Babe Ruth out of a game for cursing him. Ruth tried to fight Dinneen before the next day's game and was suspended for five days.

U.S. PRESIDENT: Ronald Reagan. As Grover Cleveland Alexander in the movie *The Winning Team*, he struck out Tony Lazzeri for all the world to see.

Frank Lovejoy, as Rogers Hornsby, hands the ball to R.R., as Grover Cleveland Alexander, in the movie The Winning Team. *Reagan, a righthander, went on to fan Tony Lazzeri.* MUSEUM OF MODERN ART, FILM STILLS ARCHIVES

CHAPTER FOUR

HALL OF SHAME

The All-Time Worst Yankees

FIRST BASE: Babe Dahlgren. In 1941 the Yankee manager, Joe McCarthy, got rid of Dahlgren, because, McCarthy said, "his arms are too short."

SECOND BASE: Phil Linz. Called "Supersub," Linz is best remembered for a brief harmonica solo on the team bus just after the Yankees had lost four straight games to the White Sox in August of 1964. "Stuff that thing!" commanded the Yankee manager, Yogi Berra. Linz tooted again, Berra charged him, and the harmonica flew. It hit Joe Pepitone in the knee, injuring him. Frank Crosetti, the Yankee shortstop-turned-coach, called this momentously insignificant incident "the worst thing I've seen in thirty-three years with the club."

SHORTSTOP: Lyn Lary. This forgotten journeyman cost Lou Gehrig the home run championship in 1931. With Lary on first base and two

out, Gehrig homered to right field. Lary thought the ball had been caught, so he rounded third and trotted into the Yankee dugout. Gehrig didn't notice, and as he trotted past third base he was called out for passing another runner. That home run would have given him forty-seven for the year; he wound up tied with Ruth for the league lead at forty-six.

THIRD BASE: Charley Smith. This is the guy the Cardinals foisted off on the Yankees in exchange for Roger Maris. The Yankees proclaimed that Smith was a budding star, but his batting average was nipped in the .220s.

OUTFIELD: Bobby Brown. George Steinbrenner was so convinced of Brown's talent that he forced the Yankee managers to play him. This paid off for Yankee Haters when Brown failed to reach Rick Monday's line drive in the seventh inning of

Babe Dahlgren, short-armed first baseman, under the critical scrutiny of Yankee manager Joe McCarthy and owner Jake Ruppert. NATIONAL BASEBALL HALL OF FAME

Good work, Lyn Lary. You cost Gehrig a home-run championship. GEORGE BRACE

Lyn Lary

the fourth game of the 1981 World Series. Brown's muff put the eventual winning runs on second and third.

OUTFIELD: George (Papa Bear) Halas. The future coach and owner of the Chicago Bears was driven to football by his brief tour with the Yankees in 1919. He managed two singles in twenty-two times up and said his proudest achievement was hitting a foul ball off Walter Johnson.

OUTFIELD: Arturo Lopez. Lopez symbolizes the media's relentless determination to make stars of even the worst Yankees. In 1965, Lopez's rookie year, *Sports Illustrated* said that he "could turn out to be the folk hero the Yankees haven't had since they captured the Italians of New York in the '30s and '40s with Lazzeri, Crosetti, Joe DiMaggio and Phil Rizzuto." Lopez's rookie year proved to be his only year. He hit .143 and became a folk hero among Yankee Haters.

CATCHER: Branch Rickey. The man who founded baseball's farm system and brought Jackie Robinson into baseball had brains, but no arm. As Yankee catcher on June 28, 1907, he allowed thirteen stolen bases, still a record. Legend has it that one runner was clearly out but the umpire was so accustomed to the "safe" signal that he couldn't change.

RIGHTHANDED PITCHER: Doyle Alexander. Another of Steinbrenner's brilliant acquisitions, Alexander pitched so poorly in the early part of the 1982 season that he punched the dugout wall in frustration, broke knuckles on his pitching hand, and missed nine weeks. He returned, but

Papa Bear Halas as a baby Yankee in 1919. CHICAGO BEARS

by August his pitching had settled into such a batting-practice groove that Steinbrenner sent him to the doctor for a physical. "I'm afraid some of our players might get hurt playing defense behind him," George said in his usual kindly manner. By the time Alexander won his first game of the 1982 season it was September, and the Yankees were scrapping with Toronto for last place. Nevertheless, Alexander's future was bright: He had three years remaining on a $2.2 million contract.

LEFTHANDED PITCHERS: Fritz Peterson and Mike Kekich. These romantic southpaws swapped wives in 1973, mocking the image of Yankee dignity and enraging the team's stuffy officials. Perhaps it would be more accurate to say that Mrs. Peterson and Mrs. Kekich traded husbands. At any rate, the Yankees quickly traded Kekich, punishing him for the un-Yankee sin of love. They kept Peterson long enough for him to lose fifteen games in 1973, then banished him to Cleveland.

RELIEF PITCHER: George Frazier. He lost three games to the Dodgers in the 1981 World Series. When told that the only other pitcher to have achieved that pinnacle was Lefty Williams, who deliberately lost three games as a member of the infamous 1919 Chicago Black Sox, Frazier commented that he hadn't *meant* to lose.

PINCH RUNNER: John Anderson. In 1904, Honest John, as he was called, stole second base with the bases loaded, a play known ever since as a "John Anderson."

DESIGNATED HITTER: Cliff Johnson. His greatest contribution to baseball was a shower-room scuffle with Goose Gossage that injured Gossage's thumb and sidelined the pitcher for much of the 1979 season.

WORST NAME: Frank Elmer (Inch) Gleich. Sorry Monk Dubiel, Bob Unglaub, Julie (Flap Ears) Wera, Ham Hyatt and Eli Grba; you didn't quite make it. For the record, Gleich played two seasons for the Yankees and hit about an inch — .133, to be exact.

MANAGER: Dick Williams. After managing the Oakland Athletics to two straight world championships, Williams was hired by the Yankees with great fanfare after the 1973 season. He never made it to spring training, as Joe Cronin, American League president, ruled that Williams was still under contract to the A's. Williams reluctantly went back to Oakland and won another world championship.

TEAM OWNER AND PRESIDENT: CBS and Mike Burke, who ran the Yankees during their Golden Era of bumbling, losing baseball from the mid '60s until (shudder) George Steinbrenner bought the team in 1973. Early in his reign, Burke wrote a smugly erudite article for *Dun's Review*, a sober and prestigious business publication, outlining the corporation's plans to bring sound business practices to baseball. By 1972, he had soundly driven the Yankees' attendance below one million, and the team was so unpopular even in New York that the Yankees had to pay to get their games broadcast on radio. CBS was in every way a fine corporate owner, and Burke should be elected to the Hall of Fame.

DESIGNATED U.S. PRESIDENT: Warren G. Harding, the first President to attend a game at

Yankee Stadium. He graced the new stadium with his presence on April 24, 1923. Appropriately enough, Harding is considered one of the worst presidents in U.S. history.

SWEET SWAPS

WHO says the Yankees are smart traders? Here's an all-star team of players the Yankees stupidly traded away.

FIRST BASE: Vic Power. One of a few blacks whom the Yankees reluctantly signed, Power was clearly ready for the major leagues in 1954. The Yankees were still lily-white, so they traded Power to the Philadelphia Athletics. He played twelve distinguished seasons in the major leagues and batted .284.

SECOND BASE: Mark Koenig. A bulwark of the Yankee powerhouses of the 1920s, Koenig was traded to Detroit in 1930, and found his way to the Chicago Cubs in time to help them win the 1932 pennant.

SHORTSTOP: Leo Durocher. The Yankees couldn't take any more Lip, so they waived him to the Reds in 1930. He starred at shortstop for the Cardinal Gas House Gang of 1934.

THIRD BASE: Clete Boyer. The Yankees thought this glove artist was washed up and traded him in 1967 to Atlanta, where he enjoyed five good seasons.

OUTFIELD: Roger Maris. The ungrateful Yankees traded their home-run king in 1967 to the Cardinals, who won two straight pennants with Maris in right field.

OUTFIELD: Lefty O'Doul. The Yanks thought O'Doul was a bad pitcher and got rid of him in 1923. He switched to the outfield and became one of baseball's best hitters, batting .398 in 1929 and finishing with a .349 lifetime average.

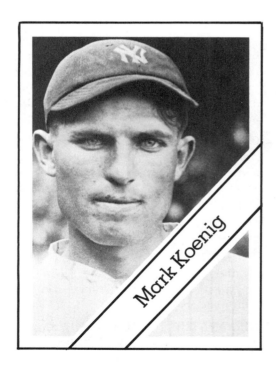

Mark Koenig

Lefty O'Doul, who got away from the Yankees before they realized he was a hitter, not a pitcher. GEORGE BRACE

33

OUTFIELD: Jackie Jensen. After the Yanks traded him in 1952, Jensen became a superb power hitter. With the Red Sox, he led the league in runs batted in three times.

CATCHER: Rick Dempsey. A scrappy player and an outstanding defensive catcher, Dempsey contributed strongly to Baltimore's 1979 pennant winners and its competitive teams of other recent years. So did pitching stars Scott McGregor and Tippy Martinez, who came from the Yankees in the same one-sided trade.

LEFTHANDED PITCHER: Larry Gura. The Yankees traded Gura to Kansas City in 1976, and two years later he pitched the Royals to the second of their three straight playoff victories over the Yankees.

RIGHTHANDED PITCHER: Lew Burdette. He was a minor leaguer when the Yankees traded him to the Milwaukee Braves in 1951, but he was a major leaguer when he beat the Yankees three games in the 1957 World Series.

Who says the Yankees know how to pick a winner? Joe McCarthy, then Yankee manager, throws his support behind Alf Landon, who needed all the help he could get. ST. LOUIS SPORTS HALL OF FAME

34

McCarthy wasn't the only Yankee who couldn't handicap a political race; Ruth's candidate couldn't even beat Herbert Hoover. NATIONAL BASEBALL HALL OF FAME

Forgotten Moments of Glory

SICK of having Yankee triumphs stuffed down your throat? Revel in these wonderful days which the Yankee propaganda machine has tried to expunge from history.

April 22, 1903 — The New York Yankees, then called the Highlanders, play their first game and are beaten by Washington, 3 to 1.

June 7, 1903 — The Yankees and Red Sox start their historic rivalry. Bill Dinneen pitches Boston to a 6 to 2 victory.

June 12, 1907 — The Yankees commit eleven errors, four of them by shortstop Kid Elberfeld, as the Detroit Tigers romp, 14 to 6.

July 15, 1907 — The Chicago White Sox crush the Yankees behind Doc White, 15 to 0.

June 30, 1908 — Cy Young lives up to his name as his no-hitter for the Red Sox beats the Yanks, 8 to 0.

June 20, 1913 — Bert Gallia, a little-known Washington pitcher, hits three of the first four Yankee batters.

September 10, 1919 — Cleveland's Ray Caldwell, a Yankee for the previous nine years, no-hits the Yankees, 3 to 0.

Opening day, 1920 — In his first game as a Yankee, Babe Ruth drops a fly ball to let in the winning runs as the Philadelphia Athletics beat the Yankees.

Cy Young. After no-hitting the Yankees, is it any wonder they named an award after him?

July 29, 1928 — The Cleveland Indians smash the Yankees, 24 to 6.

September 11, 1931 — With Ted Lyons pitching for the White Sox, Babe Ruth grounds into a triple play, Billy Sullivan to John Kerr to Lu Blue. Ruth, the third man retired on the play, is out by a mile.

35

September 9, 1932 — Yankee Frank Crosetti ties a record by striking out twice in one inning as the Yankees lose, 14 to 13.

July 7, 1936 — After losing the first three All-Star Games, the National League prevails, 4 to 3, with help from the American League's Joe DiMaggio. DiMag misses Gabby Hartnett's liner to help the National League to its first two runs, and later fumbles a single by Billy Herman to set up the game-winning run.

April 30, 1946 — Cleveland's Bob Feller pitches a no-hitter to beat the Yankees, 1 to 0, at Yankee Stadium. Frankie Hayes homers in the ninth for the only run.

May 28, 1946 — A crowd of 49,917 turns out for the first night game at Yankee Stadium, won by the Washington Senators, 2 to 1.

May 3, 1950 — Vic Raschi of the Yankees commits four balks to set an American League record.

May 4, 1950 — In a second consecutive day of glory, the Yanks fall to the White Sox and pitcher Bob Cain, 15 to 0.

September 24, 1954 — Going to their fabled bench, the Yankees send up three pinch-hitters in the ninth inning against the Athletics' Arnold Portocarrero. All three strike out; the A's win, 5 to 1. The pinchhitting immortals were Lou Berberet, Gus Triandos, and Frank Leja.

36   **October 1, 1955** — In the fourth game of the World Series, a foul ball hit by the Yankees' Don Larsen bops Yankee co-owner Del Webb on the head. He leaves, complaining of dizziness.

Larsen is the losing pitcher as the Dodgers win the game, 8 to 5.

September 21, 1956 — The Yankees leave twenty runners on base in a 13 to 9 loss to the Red Sox at Fenway Park.

September 21, 1958 — Gus Triandos, now with the Baltimore Orioles, homers for the only run as Hoyt Wilhelm, thirty-five years old, beats the Yankees on a no-hitter.

Hoyt Wilhelm as a New York Giant and first-class Yankee killer.

August 13, 1964 — CBS buys the Yankees. CBS stock drops three-eighths of a point. On NBC television news, Chet Huntley calls the deal "just one more reason to hate the Yankees."

September 25, 1966 — Attendance at Yankee Stadium sets a record low of 413 as the White Sox beat the Yankees, 4 to 1.

October 28, 1974 — Commissioner Bowie Kuhn suspends George Steinbrenner from baseball for making illegal contributions to the presidential campaign of Richard Nixon.

September 10, 1977 — The lowly Toronto Blue Jays thrash the Yankees in New York, 19 to 3.

April 30, 1982 — Gaylord Perry of Seattle beats the Yankees at Yankee Stadium for the two hundred and ninety-ninth victory of his career. Perry is forty-three years old.

May 6, 1982 — Perry becomes the fifteenth pitcher in baseball history to win 300 games, beating the Yankees at the Kingdome, 7 to 3.

July 8, 1982 — Billy Martin records his one thousandth career win as a manager as his Oakland A's beat the Yankees, 6–3.

September 17, 1982 — In an appropriate coup de grace, the Milwaukee Brewers beat the Yankees 14–0 and mathematically eliminate them from the pennant race.

Gaylord Perry, who achieved his 299th and 300th victories against the Yankees. SEATTLE MARINERS

37

CHAPTER FIVE

OFF WITH THE HALOS

The Truths Behind Yankee Myths

MYTH: The Yankees are a team of all-stars.

TRUTH: Only one Yankee, pitcher Ron Guidry, made the 1981 American League All-Star team selected by the league's players for *The Sporting News*, and only one other — left-fielder Dave Winfield — finished as high as second. Adoring broadcasters often describe journeyman Yankees such as Bucky Dent (now with Texas) and Rick Cerone as all-stars, but the players know better. Three shortstops and four catchers got enough votes to be mentioned by *The Sporting News*. Neither Dent nor Cerone were among them. In 1982, Dent was relegated to the Yankee bench — a substitute on a second division team — but he nevertheless came close to being elected by the fans as the starting shortstop on the American League All-Star team. Later in the season, this hollow symbol of the Yankee propaganda machine was traded to the Texas Rangers, and was forgotten.

MYTH: Although the Yankees of recent years have been quarrelsome and vulgar, Yankee teams of the past were models of brotherly decorum.

TRUTH: The Ruthian Yankees of the early 1920s fought and pouted continually. Wally Pipp, the first baseman, slugged Ruth in the dugout one day. Ruth's quarrels with manager Miller Huggins were at least as bitter and petty as Reggie Jackson's tiffs with Billy Martin. Ruth outweighed Huggins by a hundred pounds and, according to legend, once picked up his little manager and held him out behind a speeding train.

After Leo Durocher joined the Yankees as a young shortstop in 1928, Ruth accused him of stealing his watch. Ruth and Durocher remained enemies. Ruth and Lou Gehrig, who are always pictured in a smiling embrace, in fact were not on speaking terms during many of their Yankee years together.

Bob Shawkey, who succeeded Huggins as manager, was so antagonized by pitcher Waite Hoyt that the star righthander was traded to Detroit. As for spoiled behavior, Shawkey's successor, Joe McCarthy, observed that the Yankees of the 1930s devoted more time and energy to playing cards than to playing baseball. For shock effect, he had the clubhouse boy destroy the card table with an ax while the players looked on.

Casey Stengel took over as Yankee manager late in Joe DiMaggio's career and the two were not friendly. Stengel once sent Cliff Mapes out to replace DiMaggio in the outfield in the middle of an inning; DiMaggio waved Mapes back, and when the side was retired the great Clipper sulked into the clubhouse. He stopped speaking to Stengel thereafter.

Stengel's stars — Mickey Mantle, Whitey Ford, Yogi Berra — have been cast in history as boyishly playful. A laugh a minute, eh? Hardly. Jack Mann, who covered the team, wrote in *Sports Illustrated* that the Yankee clubhouse "held all the carefree charm of a dentist's office."

The Yankees have never been lovable. That's why generations of good Americans have hated them.

MYTH: The Yankees have always been a progressive organization.
TRUTH: The Yankees were one of the last teams to employ black players. George Weiss,

Elston Howard. Stengel called him "Eightball."

the Yankee general manager, and Casey Stengel, the manager, openly expressed their distaste for blacks. Under pressure, the Yanks finally signed a few blacks to minor-league contracts. One of them, first baseman Vic Power, led the International League in batting in 1953, and the Yankees quickly traded him to the Philadelphia Athletics for two white players. Elston Howard was the first black to make the Yankees; Stengel nicknamed him "Eightball" — and called him that to his face.

MYTH: Thurman Munson was a noble, generous and sensitive man.
TRUTH: Munson's qualities seemed to flower after his unfortunate death in 1979. When alive, he expressed frequent and profane bitterness that his contract, as fat as it was, didn't measure up to that of Reggie Jackson. Roger Angell of *The New Yorker* described Munson as "silent and scowling, possibly dangerous." In an incident described in a 1978 issue of *Sport Magazine*, a photographer said to Sparky Lyle, the Yankee relief pitcher, "He seems like a moody guy, that Munson." Lyle replied: "Nah, he's not moody, he's just mean."

MYTH: Graig Nettles was named Yankee captain in 1982. The Yankees had only two captains before him, Lou Gehrig and Thurman Munson.
TRUTH: This falsehood is repeated in an attempt to give the Yankee captaincy a sort of angelic quality, Gehrig and Munson both having suffered untimely deaths. (Indeed, the funeral wake for Gehrig is still going on, more than forty years after his death, and Munson's is just heating up.)

The Myth of the Yankee Captains isn't just limited to sentimental fans. In a nationally televised game on April 17, 1982, Nettles made an error (Good!). The announcer, Tony Kubek, who played for the Yankees and should know better, reverently intoned: "Nettles, the Yankee captain this year. Only two before him, Thurman Munson and Lou Gehrig."

In fact, Roger Peckinpaugh, a shortstop, was Yankee captain from 1914 through 1921. Babe Ruth was captain for six days in 1922, but American League officials stripped him of the post when he jumped into the stands to chase a heckler. Everett Scott, another infielder, was then named captain, and served through 1925. As if it mattered. Nobody makes a fuss about the captains of other teams. The whole subject is another disgusting example of Yankee puff.

Babe Ruth in street clothes on opening day, 1922. Ruth was under suspension then, and was suspended five times during the 1922 season, a Ruthian record that still stands. One of the suspensions cost him the Yankee captaincy. LIBRARY OF CONGRESS

MYTH: The Yankees always go first class.
TRUTH: Lou Gehrig was so underpaid during his first spring training with the Yankees that he almost took a job washing dishes. His meagre meal allowance arrived just in time to spare him that immortal indignity.

MYTH: The Yankees paid Babe Ruth handsomely even after his skills declined and promoted his image of greatness.

TRUTH: Everyone has heard of Ruth's $80,000 salary, which was then a record. He made $80,000 in 1930 and again in 1931. For 1932, the Yankees cut him to $75,000. Ruth hit .341 that season, with 41 home runs and 137 runs batted in. The grateful Yankees cut his salary to $52,000 for 1933, and to $35,000 for 1934. Ruth pleaded for an opportunity to manage the Yankees, but Edward G. Barrow, the team's business manager, not only turned him down but publicly ridiculed the idea.

MYTH: Ruth "called his shot" in the 1932 World Series against the Chicago Cubs, pointing to the center field bleachers and then hitting a home run there.

TRUTH: According to Gehrig, who was the on-deck hitter, and Gabby Hartnett, the Cub catcher, Ruth pointed not at the bleachers but at Charlie Root, the Chicago pitcher. The Cubs had been jockeying Ruth, and according to Gehrig, Ruth pointed at Root and said, "I'm going to knock the next pitch down your goddamned throat."

The Immortal Yankee Clipper knew how to keep his mouth shut.

MYTH: Joe DiMaggio was a man of modest and silent dignity.

TRUTH: DiMaggio was so vain and self-centered that he often would not deign to speak to others. Just ask the movie stars who married him. Dorothy Arnold, DiMaggio's first wife, said in her divorce action in 1944 that DiMaggio "refused to talk to me for days at a time, and several times asked me to get out of the house." Marilyn Monroe, who married DiMaggio later, complained that all he wanted to do was watch television.

In 1936, a sportswriter found himself seated in a hotel lobby near DiMaggio and teammates Frank Crosetti and Tony Lazzeri. He noticed that they were unusually quiet for three close friends and decided to time their silence. An hour and twenty minutes later, DiMaggio cleared his throat. "What did you say?" asked Crosetti. "Shut up," said Lazzeri, "he didn't say nothin'." After ten more minutes of silence, the writer could stand no more dignity and left.

MYTH: Yogi Berra was a wit.

TRUTH: Berra's few funny comments were accidental. The Yankees of that era were such a grumpy, unresponsive bunch that sportswriters grossly exaggerated Berra's humor to fill space. In *The Hustler's Handbook* (1965) Bill Veeck said this of Berra's wit: "Yogi is a completely manufactured product. He is a case study of this country's unlimited ability to gull itself and be gulled."

Berra was such a primitive fellow that his first Yankee manager, Bucky Harris, called him "Nature Boy" and "The Ape." Berra's teammates spoofed him by hanging from the dugout roof and uttering ape calls.

MYTH: Mickey Mantle had bad legs and heroically played in severe pain.

TRUTH: Mantle ignored repeated advice to improve his legs with exercise in the off-season. He preferred to play golf, riding a cart equipped with a bar. One of his historic leg injuries was suffered while playing bumper cars with golf carts on a course in Florida; Billy Martin's cart ran over Mantle's leg.

MYTH: Casey Stengel was a managerial genius, beloved by his players.

TRUTH: Stengel charmed sportswriters, but to his players he was grumpy and intolerant. When he was fired from the Yankees after twelve seasons as manager, one of his players, John Blanchard, had this to say: "He's a goddamned louse."

Not even the batboy is paying attention as Babe Ruth makes his last appearance in a major league ballpark. The empty stands at Sportsman's Park, St. Louis, were usual with the Browns playing. The master of ceremonies to Ruth's left is France Laux, a prominent sportscaster of the day.

MYTH: Babe Ruth, his voice hoarse from the cancer that soon would kill him, made his last ballpark appearance before a huge and adoring Yankee Stadium throng on June 13, 1948.

TRUTH: After appearing at Yankee Stadium, Ruth toured other major league cities. His final appearance was June 19, 1948, at Sportsman's Park, St. Louis, before a game with the woebegone Browns. Ruth talked to a largely empty stadium.

CHAPTER SIX

GREENSTRIPES

The Sheiks of Baseball

How Money, Not Brains, Built the Yankees

SPARKY ANDERSON, veteran manager of the Detroit Tigers, comments on the Yankee philosophy of team-building: "Steinbrenner has one player that's from his farm system. Everybody else they've either traded for or bought. Seventeen of our twenty-five, we raised. Steinbrenner's not breaking any rules, but as a manager I certainly couldn't look with any pride when I walked out there and I had all the great stars bought. In Detroit, if we ever win I can say, 'Hey, we came here, we built, and we won.' You know, the funny thing, the Yankees didn't win the World Series last year [1981]. They haven't walked away with too many honors, considering all the players they've been buying. I don't think of it as a magic formula. I think it's an *easy* formula. I don't see anything tough about picking up good players if you pay them enough.

Sparky Anderson, who prefers building a team to buying one. DETROIT TIGERS

45

"Players will play anywhere in the world. You'll always hear them at their press conferences say, 'Boy, I've always wanted to play in this city. I've always wanted to be a Yankee.' Yeah, they're a Yankee 'cause Mr. George just strapped a couple of Brinks trucks on 'em. I just wish some time a player would sign a big contract and stand up at a press conference and say, 'You know why I'm here, folks? Because your club put all the greenbacks on the line!'

"I don't know of any living soul who wants to go to New York City. I don't know of anybody who wants to fight that rat race when they could be in a nice, peaceful city like Cincinnati, Ohio. Who needs to go to New York City where if you walk down the street, you're running a fifty-fifty chance you might not come back? But a lot of greenbacks will get you to do a lot of things."

Hank Peters, general manager of the Balti-more Orioles and one of the most highly respected executives in baseball: "Basically, with any major league baseball team you have ticket income, which is based on the prices you charge and how many people you draw. You have concessions, which are determined by your attendance. Last is your income from broadcasting — television and radio. I would venture to say that probably for every dollar the Orioles can generate from these sources, the Yankees generate two dollars. That's because of the marketplace of New York City. You've got to face it. They're in the major market in the country. There's just no way that we or probably any other major league franchise can match what they do in New York City.

"Economically, that gives them quite an advantage. They might have a huge payroll — they do, much more than ours. They might have a much larger player development program. And generally, you'd say that operating costs in New York City are going to be higher than in Baltimore. But on the other hand, if they have twice the income that we have, even with all of these added expenses, you can see that they not only have an opportunity to come out with a large profit, but they're able to afford so many of the things that help them create a successful club on the field.

"This is a difficult thing for us to compete against. We've raised ticket prices considerably. We keep looking around, hoping there might be some untapped sources of income that we have

Hank Peters, whose Orioles consistently win despite lower salaries and earnings than the Yankees.
JERRY WACHTER: BALTIMORE ORIOLES

46

overlooked. I don't think that there are. Unfortunately, all twenty-six clubs are linked together when it comes to player contracts and salaries. The precedents established by one affect the other twenty-five. In salary arbitration, which is the most graphic example, the statistics are based on how your guy performed, but also you get into salaries. How much money is a player making with three years' experience on all twenty-six teams? How much is a five-year shortstop making? If one of them happens to be playing for a New York team or Los Angeles team or one of the others who have set a terrible precedent, you're hung. So you can have a Minnesota or a Baltimore that has a standout player, and you're faced with the salary precedents established by the clubs that can afford to do things we can't afford to do. We can't drag their salaries down, but they can drag us up to their level.

"So far, we've been able to compete. The Orioles have the best record in the American League over the last five years. The Yankees are second best. Since divisional play came into effect, the Orioles have had the best record. The Yankees are down below us. Over the last twenty-five years, the Orioles have had the best record in all of baseball. The Yankees are further down the line. So the Yankees really have not been as winning a club as the Orioles. On the other hand, because of their location they gain a lot of national publicity, and if you went before an audience and asked the question, 'Who has had the best winning record in the major leagues over the last twenty-five years?' there probably would not be too many people who would say, 'Baltimore.'

"From an operator's standpoint, you can take more pride and satisfaction in doing it our way.

The thing that you have to recognize, however, is that with the new system we have in baseball, there are different ways of building winning teams. There will still be those of us who will rely primarily on the ability to build from within and make some trades, whereas there are going to be others that will rely primarily on the free agent market. The Yankees have been doing that. They've also been investing dollars in their farm system, but thus far they appear to be using their farm-system prospects primarily to deal off to get established players. They don't want to pay the price that we sometimes have to pay to give a young player the opportunity to make that transition from being a good prospect to being a major league player.

"We all have to work very hard to use our wits a little bit more than they do. It's like going to Las Vegas to gamble. You take your life savings of $5,000 with you, and you roll the dice, and you lose it all, and you're bankrupt. On the other hand, the guy who's got a million dollars in his pocket rolls the dice and loses $5,000 and says, 'So what?' Well, the Yankees, because of their wealth, can afford to roll the dice, and if they crap out — which they do occasionally, with, say, a Don Gullett — they can just say, 'Well, we'll go on to other things.' Whereas if we roll the dice and some other clubs of lesser wealth roll the dice and lose out on a Gullett or a Don Stanhouse, it's a catastrophe for us. There's a big difference.

"So when I look to the future and ask, 'Can we continue to compete?' I don't know the answer, because I don't know how much further the salary thing can go. Oh, we can survive. But nobody just wants to be a survivor. You want to be a competitor. And if we can't compete, the enjoy-

Average Salaries

1979 RANK	1980 RANK	1981 RANK	CLUB	1981*	1980*	1979*
1	1	1	Yankees	$309,855	$242,937	$199,236
2	2	2	Phillies	289,971	221,274	197,926
21	7	3	Astros	260,789	176,720	73,660
5	4	4	Angels	259,404	191,014	155,694
8	11	5	Brewers	243,882	159,086	137,309
6	5	6	Red Sox	223,252	184,686	145,692
12	8	7	Cardinals	207,654	173,480	116,628
3	3	8	Pirates	206,359	199,185	174,439
4	9	9	Reds	201,557	162,655	165,144
17	18	10	Mets	201,303	126,488	93,607
7	12	11	Expos	195,958	158,196	142,829
19	15	12	Braves	195,449	147,989	90,366
20	24	13	White Sox	192,658	72,415	74,673
9	6	14	Dodgers	192,104	183,124	134,305
16	17	15	Indians	186,396	127,505	98,023
11	14	16	Giants	185,939	148,265	120,737
10	13	17	Rangers	178,131	148,792	128,806
15	19	18	Orioles	169,919	116,156	101,266
24	21	19	Tigers	160,561	86,998	63,377
26	26	20	A's	148,065	54,994	41,220
13	10	21	Cubs	125,117	160,209	104,116
18	20	22	Royals	112,910	100,453	91,583
14	16	23	Padres	103,106	138,978	103,819
23	25	24	Blue Jays	97,271	67,218	67,044
25	22	25	Mariners	95,263	82,244	61,830
22	23	26	Twins	85,736	80,358	70,703
Average Salary.............................				185,651	143,756	113,558

*Salary figures have been discounted for salary deferrals without interest, at a rate of 9 percent per year for the period of delayed payments.

ment will go out of it for a lot of the fans in this country."

Things may be worse than Peters thought. According to *Broadcast Magazine*, the Orioles were paid $1.05 million in 1982 for television and radio rights. The Yankees were paid $6 million.

Peter Gammons, the *Boston Globe*'s veteran baseball writer, posed the issue this way in an early 1982 edition of *The Sporting News*: "What's the future of competitive balance when the Yankees will have a payroll of $13 million in 1982 and the Seattle Mariners will probably have gross revenues of $6 million?" As things turned out, the poor Mariners and rich Yankees played about evenly in 1982.

Thanks to the Major League Baseball Players Association, we can see just how blatantly the Yankees have used their wealth. Every season, the association tabulates the mean player salary, team by team. Opposite are the rankings for 1979, 1980 and 1981.

And still they lose! Hallelujah! Look at 1981. The average Yankee made $309,855. That was $117,751 more than the average Dodger, but the Dodgers won the World Series. In 1980, the Kansas City Royals, a hand-to-mouth bunch averaging only $100,453, humbled the overstuffed Yankees, who were making nearly two-and-a-half times as much per player.

Want to go back another year? In 1979, the Baltimore Orioles romped to the American League East pennant with players who were making an average of $101,266. The average Yankee made nearly twice as much — and his team finished fourth.

And yet New York writers and broadcasters

Catfish Hunter, the first million-dollar man on Steinbrenner's greenstripes.

still admonish us to admire the Yankee management for its use of money, if not for its character, and to respect the players as "professionals." That they are. Like King Saud.

Before George Steinbrenner came along, the highest-paid baseball player was Dick Allen of the Chicago White Sox at $250,000. Then, after the 1973 season, pitcher Catfish Hunter was declared a free agent, and signed with the Yanks. Here's what Steinbrenner paid him:

> $100,000 as a bonus for signing;
> $100,000 a year for five years as a player, and then for fifteen more years in retirement;
> $250,000 more in deferred salary at $50,000 a year for five years;
> $200,000 in lawyer's fees;
> A $750,000 life insurance policy for himself, and $25,000 policies for both of his two children;
> A new car every year.

Hunter's contract came to $3,350,000. Averaged out over the five seasons that it covered, that's $670,000 a year, or $51,538.46 for each of the sixty-five games that Hunter won for the Yankees.

Think that's gross? Here's what George gave Reggie Jackson in 1977:

> A bonus of $400,000;
> $200,000 a year for five years;
> $132,000 a year for five additional years in deferred salary;
> $40,000 a year for fifteen years thereafter for public relations duties; (Is Jackson now improving the Yankees' public relations by playing for the California Angels?)
> A loan of $250,000 at six percent interest, a subsidized rate. (Why in the world did Reggie Jackson need a *loan*?)

Goose Gossage got $2,748,000, including a $750,000 bonus. Rawly Eastwick, another relief pitcher, joined George for $1.1 million and didn't pan out. Neither did Don Gullett, a starting pitcher whom Steinbrenner paid $2.1 million. But what's an odd million or three?

George lured Luis Tiant from Boston for a two-year contract totaling $740,000 and Tommy John from the Dodgers for a three-year total of $1,417,000. John, who is always depicted in the media as a fine, unselfish and religious man, invoked a contract technicality in the spring of 1982 and coerced a raise, no doubt so he could increase his church pledge. Even that proved inadequate; by midseason, after he'd been temporarily relegated to the bullpen, John was petulantly demanding to be traded. He was swapped to the California Angels, who were willing to pay his bloated salary because they were in a pennant race and badly needed pitching help.

Not counting odds and ends of half a million or so, that brings us to Dave Winfield's momentous ten-year contract, which brought Winfield into greenstripes in 1981. According to the *New York Times*, Winfield's contract could earn him as much as $22,473,763, assuming ten percent raises to reflect the cost of living. Winfield gets a cost-of-living raise every other year. Here's his take, assuming those ten percent raises:

> A $1 million bonus for signing;
> 1981 — $1,400,000;
> 1982 and 1983 — $1,540,000;
> 1984 and 1985 — $1,863,400;
> 1986 and 1987 — $2,254,714;
> 1988 and 1989 — $2,728,204;
> 1990 — $3,301,127;
> Annual bonuses of $25,000 for playing in 130 or more games, $25,000 for winning a Gold Glove award for defense, and $50,000 for winning the Most Valuable Player award.
> The Yankees have the right to buy out the final two years at half the salary.

For 1982, the Yankees added two outfielders from Cincinnati — Ken Griffey for six years at $6.25 million, and Dave Collins for three years at $2,475,000. If the Yanks want Griffey for a seventh year, he gets an additional $1.1 million; if they don't, he gets $250,000 as a farewell gift. If Collins is wanted beyond three years, he'll get $700,000 each for the fourth and fifth years, or goodbye kisses of $350,000 for the fourth year and $175,000 for the fifth. Griffey, however, took until late August to warm up, and Collins never found a niche for himself with the revolving-door Yankees of '82.

So Steinbrenner traded Collins to Toronto — just another million-dollar mistake — then signed free-agent sluggers Don Baylor and Steve Kemp, and pitcher Bob Shirley to contracts totaling more than $10 million. The poor Orioles tried to sign Kemp, but Steinbrenner outbid them by $200,000 a year, again asserting his only kind of superiority.

Sparky Anderson, I think you had something.

CHAPTER SEVEN

A TRAIL OF SLIME

George Steinbrenner and the Yankee Tradition

CRITICS have accused George Steinbrenner of being mean, crooked, pompous, conniving, greedy, grasping, overbearing, intrusive, offensive in his displays of wealth, cruelly critical of his managers and players, destructive to his own team, and an affront to the Yankee tradition.

That's unfair. Steinbrenner is squarely in line with the Yankee tradition. In some ways, he may be an improvement.

The Yankees were founded in 1903 by Frank Farrell, a bartender turned gambler, and William S. (Big Bill) Devery, another barkeep who worked his way up — to chief of police.

Farrell sat with Devery in a box behind the Yankee dugout and endlessly harassed his managers and players. After games, he would storm into the clubhouse and criticize the manager's strategy and the players' performance.

Sound familiar?

The Yankee owners went through managers like…well, like another Yankee owner we all know. Clark Griffith, a former pitching star and a man of great baseball intelligence, quit in disgust during the 1908 season after managing the Yankees for five years. George Stallings, who would later gain fame as manager of the Miracle Boston Braves of 1914, had the Yankees in first place in 1910, but he quarreled violently with Farrell and Devery and was fired. The Yankees fell to second place.

Hal Chase, the next manager, was a curious choice. He was the Yankee first baseman and was widely suspected of throwing games — a shameful form of moonlighting, to be sure, but in those days no one was willing to pay a Yankee for posing in Jordache jeans.

Chase was not convicted — Steinbrenner is one up in that regard. As to loyalty, one of those deeply-rooted Yankee virtues, Chase had jumped the team in 1908 to play outlaw ball on

Harry Wolverton, who managed the Yankees to a glorious last-place finish in 1912, should be happy to be facing his owner, Frank Farrell; after all, if Steinbrenner had owned the team then, Wolverton would never have made it past June. LIBRARY OF CONGRESS

the West Coast. He had returned to the Yankees, but his teammates disliked him even before he was named manager.

Prince Hal, as he was called, brought the Yankees home sixth in 1911 and was fired. His replacement, one Harry Wolverton, arrived for spring training in 1912 wearing a sombrero and proclaiming that the Yanks would win the pennant. Instead, they finished last, and Wolverton, too, was sacked.

That brought on Frank Chance, known as the Peerless Leader for managing the Chicago Cubs to four pennants. Chance was deaf in one ear, and while he raged at his players from the dugout bench, Chase — still the team's first baseman — sat on his deaf side and mimicked him for the players' amusement. When Chance finally caught on, he ordered Chase out of uniform and traded him to the White Sox that very night for third baseman Rollie Zeider, who had a crippling bunion, and Babe Borton, a subpar first baseman. "Chase traded for a bunion and an onion," proclaimed the *New York Globe*. The owners were furious with Chance, who in turn tried to slug

Devery. That was the last straw. Chance was gone, and Roger Peckinpaugh, the team's shortstop, was named manager.

The first seeds of the Yankee tradition had been richly sown. Players maligned, managers fired, crime suspected, tension, conflict, mistreatment of decent men and elevation of others ...ah, the glorious pinstripes.

But Farrell and Devery couldn't afford the kind of crass greed for which the Yankees would later become famous. In fact, they could barely afford to die: Farrell left an estate of $1,072, while Devery left debts of $1,023. The next owners added a richer ingredient.

They had plenty of it. Jacob Ruppert, a bachelor aristocrat who employed a valet and collected jades and porcelains, had inherited a profitable brewery. His partner, Tillinghast L'Hommedieu Huston, was a self-made man who liked to pal around with athletes — a jock-sniffer, in modern parlance. Both men made a practice of visiting the Yankee clubhouse and second-guessing their manager after losses.

Ruppert and Huston fought each other, too, much like Steinbrenner and his tortured subordinates. While Huston was serving overseas in World War I, Ruppert hired Miller Huggins to manage the Yanks, although he knew that Huston disapproved. Thereafter, Huston carped constantly at Huggins and finally sold his share of the team to Ruppert.

But the mark Ruppert made on the Yankees and baseball was deep green. The Yankees' famous pennants of the 1920s were outright purchases.

From the Philadelphia Athletics, Ruppert

bought Bob Shawkey, an ace pitcher, for $85,000, and Frank (Home Run) Baker, a star third baseman, for $35,000. That prompted Carl Mays, a fine pitcher for the Boston Red Sox, to become the first player to openly salivate for Yankee money. Mays struck a pout, demanded to be traded to the Yankees, and walked out. Ruppert bought him. Ban Johnson, the American League president, was outraged, and barred the deal, just as Commissioner Bowie Kuhn would bar the Yankees' purchase of pitcher Vida Blue more than a half-century later. But the Yankees took Johnson to court, won the case, and got Mays.

Then came The Big One. After the 1919 season, the Red Sox owner, Harry Frazee, was being hounded for money by two men. One was Joe Lannin, who had sold the Red Sox to Frazee on credit and wanted his money. The other was Babe Ruth, an outstanding young pitcher who had switched to the outfield and electrified baseball in 1919 by hitting twenty-nine home runs; the previous major league record had been twenty-four. Ruth was making $10,000 a year and wanted $20,000.

Instead, Frazee sold Ruth to the greedy Yankees for $100,000 — in its time an amount as breathtaking as any of Steinbrenner's free-agent contracts. Moreover, the Yankees loaned Frazee $300,000 and *took a mortgage on Fenway Park as collateral.*

Still the Yankees didn't win, so Ruppert bought more players from the Red Sox. In 1921, the Yanks finally won a pennant. In 1922, they won another, acquiring third baseman Joe Dugan from Boston in the middle of the season to do it.

By 1923, when the Yankees won their third

straight pennant, eleven of their players had come from the poor Red Sox. The Yankees won ninety-eight games that season, and ninety-seven of them were won by pitchers whom the Yanks had bought or acquired in one-sided trades. Not even Steinbrenner has challenged that record, although he has tried.

When challenged with truth, sophisticated Yankee fans acknowledge that money had something to do with Yankee successes of the 1920s. But they insist that the Yankee champions of the '30s and '40s resulted from intelligence, unselfish virtue, healthy nutritional practices, and, most of all, the great Yankee farm system.

The Yankee farm system did produce excellent players — but not enough to win. The Yankees bought the rest. Their two star pitchers of the '30s, Lefty Gomez and Red Ruffing, were outright purchases. Gomez came from the San Francisco Seals for $35,000, Ruffing from the Red Sox for $50,000 and outfielder Cedric Durst. (Who would want a player with a name like Cedric Durst?)

Frank Crosetti, the shortstop, was purchased. So was Joe DiMaggio, a bargain at $50,000 from San Francisco. Tommy Henrich, who starred alongside DiMaggio in the Yankee outfield, was baseball's first free agent. He was in the Cleveland farm system, and Commissioner Kenesaw Mountain Landis declared in 1937 that the Indians had violated Henrich's contractual rights. The Yankees — then as now baseball's richest

Red Ruffing, bought by the Yankees for $50,000.

team, thanks to the accident of location — outbid the field for Henrich's services.

Ah, truth. It's enough to send a Yankee fan reeling off to get a Reggie Bar or a cup of Mr. Coffee.

The Yankee champions of the 1950s are recalled as the team of Casey Stengel, Mickey Mantle, Whitey Ford and Yogi Berra, whose praises will not be sung in this book. But they were also the team of Ewell Blackwell, Jim Konstanty, Johnny Hopp, Enos Slaughter, Johnny Mize and Sal Maglie — all veteran stars whom the Yankees bought.

Not that the Yankees were generous. George Weiss, a master at devious and petty acts, was promoted to Yankee general manager in 1948, and his first important acquisition was slugger Mize, purchased from the New York Giants in late August of 1949. The price was $40,000 plus another $25,000 if Mize helped the Yankees win the pennant. The trusting Giants left that judgement up to Weiss, who in October faced this problem of logic:

The Yankees won the pennant by one game. Mize's hitting won two games during the pennant race and another in the World Series. Did Mize help the Yankees win?

Weiss's answer: No.

Weiss didn't trust his players to lead clean lives, so he hired private detectives to follow them

Tommy Henrich, the first free agent lured by Yankee wealth. GEORGE BRACE

at night. Cheap private detectives, at that: The one who followed Bobby Richardson, Tony Kubek and Elston Howard wore a purple suit and white sneakers.

Weiss's nemesis among major league owners was Bill Veeck, who at various times owned the Cleveland Indians, St. Louis Browns and Chicago White Sox. Veeck was Weiss's opposite — a cheerful, friendly and generous man without much money. He called Weiss a "fugitive from the human race" and enjoyed baiting him. The two men happened to share the podium at a baseball dinner after the 1948 season when Weiss was engaged in delicate contract negotiations with Joe DiMaggio. Weiss was offering $85,000. Veeck took the microphone and suggested that $200,000 would be a fair offer. Weiss stormed off the podium.

Weiss fired Bucky Harris, a popular manager who had been told that he would be rehired for 1949, and engaged Casey Stengel to take his place. Weiss and Stengel were old friends, and Stengel managed the Yankees to ten pennants and seven world championships in twelve seasons. Then Weiss fired him.

Weiss even fired Mel Allen and Red Barber, the famous broadcasters. In August of 1956, he decided it was time to get rid of Phil Rizzuto, who for years had starred at shortstop for the Yankees. Weiss wanted the kiss of death to be soft, but instead he made it torturous. He told Rizzuto that someone had to be cut, and asked the thirty-eight-year-old veteran for suggestions. One by one, Rizzuto suggested players the team could do without; Weiss disagreed. Rizzuto finally caught on, and Weiss confirmed the bad news. Rizzuto left the clubhouse in tears.

We should not shine the unkind light of reality on Weiss without similarly illuminating the career of Edward Grant Barrow, Yankee business manager from 1920 to 1939, president from 1939 to 1945, and chairman from 1945 to 1947. Barrow's official portrait glows with dignity, and the Yankee propaganda machine has installed him in history as a baseball executive of uncommon wisdom and vision.

In his role as gentleman, Barrow once knocked sportswriter Bill Slocum across a desk because he disapproved of something Slocum had written. He also disapproved of smoking by women and once made a Yankee Stadium employee order a woman in the grandstand to put out her cigarette.

Barrow did not disapprove of saving money. After DiMaggio hit .357 with thirty home runs in 1941 — the season of his fifty-six-game hitting streak — Barrow asked him to take a pay cut and publicly compared DiMaggio's salary to a soldier's pay of twenty-one dollars a month. Dirty pool, but it worked; DiMaggio settled for a small raise, and endured piles of hate mail inspired by Barrow's comments.

As Man of Vision, we need only quote Barrow. He was manager of the Red Sox in 1919, when Babe Ruth was electrifying baseball with his first great home-run season. Barrow spoke these prophetic words: "After Babe has satisfied himself by hanging up a record for home runs that never will be touched, he will become a .400 hitter. He wants to establish a record of thirty or thirty-five home runs this year, and when he has done that he will start getting a lot of base hits that will win us more games than his home runs. He will just meet the ball and hit to left field as well as Ty Cobb. He will not be trying to knock the ball out of the lot after this season. He will be content with his record because it will be far and away out of the reach of any other player the game is likely to develop."

By 1944, most major league teams had installed lights for night play. Not the Yankees. Barrow called night baseball "a wart on the nose of the game." He later elaborated: "I am more convinced than ever that there is absolutely no future in electric-lighted play. It killed the minors. It has ruined thousands of fine prospects. It has chased the youngsters out of our parks. It has deteriorated the living habits of players and spectators."

Two years later, lights were installed at Yankee Stadium.

With this noble tradition, why don't the local fans appreciate George Steinbrenner? It is a question that Steinbrenner himself often asks.

THE ALL-TIME BOUGHT YANKEES

FIRST BASE: Tommy Henrich (*Sorry, Tom, no room in the outfield. You should have stayed with the Indians.*)

SECOND BASE: Joe Dugan (*Another switch, but Dugan wasn't called Jumping Joe for nothing.*)

SHORTSTOP: Bucky Dent

THIRD BASE: Frank (Home Run) Baker

LEFT FIELD: Dave Winfield

CENTER FIELD: Joe DiMaggio

RIGHT FIELD: Babe Ruth

CATCHER: Reggie Jackson (*Well, we didn't have a catcher and can you think of anyone else you'd rather see quiver behind the mask?*)

LEFT-HANDED DESIGNATED HITTER: Johnny Mize (*Go practice your bunting, Murcer.*)

RIGHT-HANDED DESIGNATED HITTER: Bob Watson

RIGHT-HANDED PITCHER: Red Ruffing (*With Catfish Hunter a close second.*)

LEFT-HANDED PITCHER: Lefty Gomez (*You may be richer, Tommy John, but Gomez was better.*)

RELIEF PITCHER: Goose Gossage

Lefty Gomez, another purchased pinstriper.

CHAPTER EIGHT

Great Yankee Humiliations

MOST baseball history has been written by and for Yankee fans. "The history of the New York Yankees is virtually the history of baseball," gloats Dave Anderson, a New Yorker, in the very first sentence of a typically parochial work entitled *The Yankees: The Four Fabulous Eras of Baseball's Most Famous Team*, published in 1979 by Random House, New York (where else?).

In fact, baseball's finest moments *have* concerned the Yankees — in defeat. These episodes of glory have brightened the face of America ever since the Yankees played their first game, on April 22, 1903, and lost, 3 to 1, to the Washington Senators.

In 1904, the Yankees (then called the Highlanders) engaged in their first pennant race. Trailing Boston by one game on the final day of the season, the Yankees hosted the Pilgrims (that was their name) in a doubleheader.

Chesbro on the Mound

Everything looked rosy for the New York nine that day,
The Highlanders were one game back, with two games left to play.
Chesbro was the pitcher the New Yorkers came to cheer,
They called him Happy Jack, and he was having quite a year.

He had started fifty games and completed forty-seven.
He had won forty-one and lost only eleven.
And when Happy Jack came to bat and tripled in the third
The hats came off; the New York fans thundered like a herd.

But Bill Dinneen of Boston pitched, and Chesbro didn't score
And neither team could plate a run through inning number four.
In the New York fifth, the home team took a two-to-nothing lead,
Then Jimmy Williams, bless his heart, performed a gracious deed.
This Highlander, at second base, immortalized his name
By throwing wildly home, letting Boston tie the game.
Chesbro stopped the rally, and the fans let out a cheer,
They knew that Happy Jack would bring the pennant home this year.

In the Boston ninth, Lou Criger singled. Could he ever score?
Not with Chesbro pitching. Happy Jack would close the door.
A bunt moved Criger up one base, but the fans were never frightened.
They knew they were New Yorkers, and they knew they were enlightened.
So when Criger dashed to third on a pitiful ground ball,
The fans and Chesbro stood as one, lords above the brawl.
After all, two men were out, and the batter shook with fear
And Chesbro smiled and scratched and spat and looked forward to a beer.

There was ease in Chesbro's manner as he looked down to the plate.
He scorned the Pilgrim batter, who regarded him with hate.
So Jack wound up and wheeled around, and his pitch flew like a bird,
The catcher's mitt stabbed out, and Criger yelled and dashed from third.
Oh, elsewhere in this favored land the sun is shining bright,
Children laugh, and grownups cheer and crickets chirp at night.
In the history of America, we reserve a sacred niche
For that moment back in nineteen-four: Chesbro's great wild pitch.

Outfielder Patrick Maloney — part of the proud Yankee tradition, circa 1912 — would fit right in on the woebegone Yankee bench of the 1980s.
LIBRARY OF CONGRESS

From second place in 1904, the Yankees sank. They hit bottom in 1908, losing 103 games, and finished last again in 1912, 55 games out of first place. Their owners, a pair of sleazy pols, harped constantly at the players and fired one manager after another (sound familiar?). In 1913 they made the mistake of hiring Frank Chance, the former Cub first baseman (as in Tinker to Evers to Chance) who knew enough about his old position to evaluate the play of Hal Chase, who had been playing first base for the Yankees since 1905. Chance told a sportswriter that Chase was throwing games; he was known to be involved with gamblers. The Great Blackstripes Scandal, as it was never called, was brushed over; the newspaper reported only that Chase didn't seem to be playing extra hard. Unlike the infamous Chicago Black Sox of 1919, Chase was never caught in his transgressions.

The Yankees got caught in their first World Series in 1921. Babe Ruth had hit fifty-nine home runs, but John McGraw, the Giant manager, told his pitcher, Art Nehf, to bait the Babe. "Hey Babe, I'm gonna throw you a big lollypop curve," Nehf shouted. He did; Ruth swung and missed. Nehf repeated the taunt and the pitch, and Ruth repeated his fruitless swing. Nehf fanned Ruth three times that day. Ruth also gounded out to end the Series, won by the Giants five games to three.

The Yankees bought more players the next season, won another pennant, and lost another World Series to the Giants, this one a glorious four-game sweep. Nehf fanned Ruth on four pitches in the first inning of the first game, and the Bambino got all of two hits the rest of the way.

Had you read about that sweep? Had anyone told you about the heroics of Heinie Groh, the Giant third baseman with the odd bottle-shaped bat, who clobbered Yankee pitching at a .474 clip? Probably not; a World Series like that doesn't fit the heroic Yankee mold into which baseball history is poured. But the 1926 World Series featured a drama of such high moment that no one could ignore it.

Yankee Stadium; the seventh game. The underdog Cardinals, under Rogers Hornsby, tied the Series the day before as Grover Cleveland Alexander — thirty-nine years old, alcoholic

and epileptic, deaf in one ear from shelling during World War I — beat the Yankees for the second time.

The Cardinals led 3 to 2 in the final game, but the Yankees loaded the bases in the seventh. With slugger Tony Lazzeri up, Hornsby pulled pitcher Jess Haines and beckoned Alexander from the bull pen.

LES BELL, the Cardinal third baseman: "I can see him yet, to this day, walking in from the left-field bull pen through the gray mist. He just came straggling along, a lean old Nebraskan, wearing a Cardinal sweater, his face wrinkled, that cap sitting on top of his head and tilted to one side — that's the way he liked to wear it.

"When Alec reached the mound, Rog handed him the ball and said, 'There's two out and they're drunk' — meaning the bases were loaded — 'and Lazzeri's the hitter.'

"'Okay,' Alec said. 'I'll tell you what I'm gonna do. I'm gonna throw the first one inside to him, fast.'

"'No, no,' Rog said. 'You can't do that.'

"Alec nodded his head very patiently and said, 'Yes, I can. Because if I do and he swings at it he'll most likely hit it on the handle, or if he does hit it good it'll go foul. Then I'm going to come outside with my breaking pitch.'

"Rog looked him over for a moment, then gave

Grover Cleveland Alexander — then a thirty-nine-year-old alcoholic epileptic who was deaf in one ear — still had what it took to put away Lazzeri and the Yanks in game seven of the 1926 World Series.

63

Alec a slow smile and said, 'Who am I to tell *you* how to pitch?'

"So we all went back to our positions and Alec got set to work. He had gone nine the day before, and if he got out of this jam he still had two more innings to go today. He was nearly forty years old — but doggone, there wasn't another man in the world I would have rather seen out there at that moment than Grover Cleveland Alexander.

"When you hear those stories about how Alec was out all night celebrating and how he was hung over when he came in, it's a lot of bunk. He came in there cold, took eight warmup pitches and he was ready.

"Alec was a little bit of the country boy psychologist out on that mound. He knew it was Lazzeri's rookie year, and that here it was, seventh game of the World Series, two out and the bases loaded and the score 3–2. Lazzeri *had* to be anxious up there. And don't think when Alec walked in it wasn't slower than ever — he wanted Lazzeri to stand up there as long as possible, thinking about the situation. And he just *knew* Tony's eyes would pop when he saw that fastball.

"Sure enough, the first pitch to Lazzeri is the fastball in tight, not a strike. Well, Tony jumped at it and hit the hell out of it, a hard drive down the left field line. Now for fifty years that ball has been travelling. It has been foul anywhere from an inch to twenty feet, depending on who you're listening to or what you're reading. But I was standing on third base and I'll tell you — it was foul all the way. All the way.

"And then you should have seen Tony Lazzeri go after two breaking balls on the low outside corner of the plate. He couldn't have hit them

with a ten-foot pole. Then Alec shuffled off the mound toward the dugout.

"Alec handled them like babies in the eighth, one, two, three, just like he knew he had to. In the bottom of the ninth they had their good hitters coming up — Combs, Koenig, Ruth, then Meusel and Gehrig.

"Combs led off. He hit a doggone ball down to me and I got it in between hops and threw him out. Then Koenig came up and *he* hit one down to me off the end of the bat, spinning like crazy. I went to my right, picked it up and threw *him* out.

"So Ruth came up with two out and nobody on, just as Alec had wanted it. He took Babe to a full count and then lost him on a low outside pitch that wasn't off by more than an eyelash.

"Ruth got to first and then, for some reason I've never been able to figure out, tried to steal second. Bob O'Farrell gunned the ball down to Hornsby, Rog slapped on the tag and that was it.

"We all froze for a second, then rushed at Alec. We surrounded him, the whole team did, and pounded him around pretty good. He kept nodding his head and smiling and saying very softly, 'Thanks, boys, thanks.' So many other things have come and gone now through the years. It's a long time ago, isn't it? But whenever I think of Alec walking in from left field through the mist, it seems like yesterday. I can see him yet..."

Of the World Series played from 1929 through 1935, you, if a casual baseball fan, may have heard only about the 1932 Series, in which Ruth supposedly "called his shot," pointing to the center field bleachers in Chicago's Wrigley Field and then hitting a home run there. In fact, Ruth's called shot is a myth, and the six World Series surrounding 1932 were better events — because the Yankees were not in them.

In six of those seasons the supposedly powerful Yankees were overpowered, three times by Connie Mack's Philadelphia Athletics and twice by the Detroit Tigers. The other team that stuck the pinstripes was the 1933 Washington Senators, a patched-together squad of veterans whose playing manager, Joe Cronin, was the youngest man in the lineup at twenty-six. Cronin's veterans included catcher Luke Sewell, who played an unusual role.

SEWELL recalled their relationship: "Joe Cronin came to me in the spring of the year, and he said, 'Luke, I don't know anything about pitching. I want you to help me with the pitching.'

"I said, 'In what respect?' He said, 'Well, tell me when you think a man begins to weaken, and when we should change pitchers.'

"Nobody on the club knew about it except Cronin and me. When I picked up dirt and threw it toward first base, he started a man warming up. When I picked up dirt and threw it toward Cronin at shortstop, he took the pitcher out. We did it all year long, and during the World Series."

The Yankees and Senators fought all season, literally as well as in a sporting sense, and the Senators won the pennant by beating the Yankees fourteen times in twenty-two meetings.

CRONIN vividly remembered two climactic plays: "We were behind one to nothing. Buddy Myer was at bat, and he hit a foul ball just right close to the screen. Bill Dickey, the

Joe Cronin, Hall of Fame shortstop who managed the Senators to a pennant in 1933 and the Red Sox to one in 1946. BOSTON RED SOX

Yankee catcher, went back and caught it. But the umpire, Bill McGowan, ruled that the ball had just barely skimmed the screen. Myer hit the next pitch out of the ball park, and we won, 2 to 1.

"This other crazy game, we were ahead 7 to 4, but the Yankees had Lou Gehrig on second base and Dixie Walker on first. Tony Lazzeri hit a ball to right center — hit it pretty good. There was a little bank in the outfield, and the ball ricocheted against that bank and came back, and Goose Goslin caught it in front of the bleachers. When the ball was hit, Gehrig played it safe. He didn't run, but Dixie Walker did. So when Gehrig finally started running he was just on one side of second base and Walker was on the other. Walker could run faster, and he had to slow up.

"They both rounded third at the same time. Art Fletcher, the third-base coach, couldn't do anything, so he let them both go in. I went out for the relay in right-center and turned around and threw it home. Luke Sewell caught the ball and tagged them both out — one, two! Did I get two assists? No; that's an assist they owe me."

If the Detroit infield of 1934 and 1935 had played in New York, it would be the most famous in history. In 1934, first baseman Hank Greenberg drove in 139 runs, second baseman Charlie Gehringer drove in 127, shortstop Billy Rogell drove in 100, and third baseman Marv Owen, the weakling among the four, drove in 96. Altogether, they produced 462 runs batted in and 258 extra-base hits. And this was an infield known for its *defense*.

The Tigers also picked up Goose Goslin, who drove in 100 runs himself both seasons, and Mickey Cochrane, their catcher and manager. The pitching was good, too — Schoolboy Rowe, Tommy Bridges, Eldon Auker, General Crowder, and the wonderfully nicknamed Firpo Marberry. Four members of that team are in the Hall of Fame, none more notable than Gehringer. Can you imagine having the best defensive second baseman in the league — and have him turn in batting averages of .356, .330, .354 and .371? That was Gehringer, 1934 through 1937 — the year he finally beat Lou Gehrig for the batting championship.

Beginning in 1936, a dark age settled on baseball. By the fall of 1942, the Yankees had won five World Series in six seasons and seemed poised to win another. Their opponents were the eager but inexperienced St. Louis Cardinals — surely no match for a seasoned Yankee team that included Joe DiMaggio, Charlie Keller, Bill Dickey, Phil Rizzuto and Joe Gordon, plus pitching aces Ernie Bonham, Spud Chandler, Hank Borowy and Red Ruffing.

Who were these St. Louis bumpkins anyway? A roughneck named Slaughter, a couple of green rookies named Musial and Kurowski, a skinny shortstop named Marion — who were these guys?

By the ninth inning of the first game, it appeared that they were the usual October patsies. Ruffing sailed into the ninth with a one-hitter and a 7 to 0 lead. The Cardinals exploded for four runs in the ninth and loaded the bases for Musial with two out. "They put Chandler in because he was a sinker-ball pitcher, a ground-ball pitcher," Musial recalls, "and sure enough, I grounded out to first base."

The Cardinals jumped in front 3 to 0 in the second game, but in the eighth the Yankees got to John Beazley — a rookie pitcher, for heaven's sake, trying to beat the mighty Yankees. DiMaggio singled a run home and Keller followed with a homer to tie the game.

Surely the Cardinals would die. Bonham, the American League's leading pitcher that season at 21 and 5, got the first two Cardinals in the home eighth, although Terry Moore tested DiMaggio with a drive to deep center.

But then Slaughter doubled, and Musial singled him home. What's this?

The Yankee ninth. Roll the drums. Dickey singled. Tuck Stainback ran for Dickey. Buddy Hassett grounded a single to right — just the kind of hit that moves a runner to third.

Without looking at Stainback, let alone a cut-off man, Slaughter charged the ball, grabbed it on the run, and fired it to Kurowski at third. Stainback was an easy out, and Beazley retired the next two batters to win the game.

"The throw that broke the Yankees' back," they called it. But that was later. Now the Series moved to Yankee Stadium — a strange and ominous place to the young Cardinals, or so the New York writers thought. Who, for example, could patrol the distant reaches of center field with the great DiMaggio?

Terry Moore, for one. With two out and a man on in the home sixth, DiMaggio hit a drive in the left-center gap, and both Musial and Moore went for it, leaving neither in position to chase the ball if it got through. Musial hit the ground to avoid a collision. Inside-the-park home run? Not quite;

Moore dived over Musial and caught the ball.

The next Yankee batter, leading off the home seventh, was Gordon, the American League's most valuable player. He smashed a ball toward the left-field stands. Running back for it was Musial, a slender youngster new to the outfield. He leaped and caught the ball.

Now Keller, with the Yankees still just a run back. His shot to right might go over — might go over — but it was Slaughter's turn. Half jumping and half climbing the wall, he pulled it down.

Three home run bids, three Cardinal outfielders, three outs. A shaky shutout for young Ernie White as the Cardinals won, 2 to 0. They thrashed the Yankees 9 to 6 the next day, and in the fifth game Kurowski homered in the ninth for a 4 to 2 lead.

The Yankees' last stand. Gordon singled, and second baseman Jimmy Brown muffed Dickey's grounder. Were the Cardinals shaking? Would the Yankees finally humiliate the presumptuous Beazley?

MARTY MARION recalls: "It was the last of the ninth inning. There were men on first and second with nobody out. Jerry Priddy was the hitter. The bunt was in order.

"When you're defending on a bunt play, you play close to the runner to hold him on, and then you try to back off in a way so he thinks you're going to stay in position. You're trying to decoy the guy so he will take too big a lead. He wants to break far enough off second base so he can beat the throw to third on a bunt, and he's very susceptible to a good pickoff. I had a knack of getting back of the runner pretty good. We picked off a heck of a lot of 'em. We were good at it.

67

Marty Marion, a sneaky young shortstop who picked off the American League's Most Valuable Player in the 1942 World Series. ST. LOUIS CARDINALS

"It wasn't a set play. It was a play that just happens. The pitch to Priddy was high and inside. He backed off, and Walker Cooper, our catcher, came up throwing. I got behind Gordon and we had him good. We had him picked off *so far*. It wasn't a close play at all.

"Gordon knocked me down, and his cap flew off. Yep, he had a bald spot. We used to call him 'Skinhead.'

"We were not awed by the famous Yankees, although we knew they had a good ball club. We were a very cocky bunch, and we knew very well that they could not beat us, because we had the best team that the Cardinals ever had. We had great pitching, great defense, speed and good hitting.

"The whole time we were in the Series, every time we came into the clubhouse we started figuring up how much money we were going to make. Even after the first game, we were figuring what the winner's share would be. Terry Moore, our captain and our great center fielder, kept saying, 'Marty, Marty, you all quit talking about money. That's bad luck.' I said, 'Heck it is. We're gonna beat 'em easy.' We had a ball club that had just come down the stretch red hot, won the most games a Cardinal team's ever won. Nobody could beat us. Just because we played the Yankees, we didn't think they could beat us either.

"I think the winner's share turned out to be $6,192. Biggest check I ever saw. I was making $5,000, so it was a check bigger than we got all season. The players today would scoff at it."

ENOS SLAUGHTER, who closed his career as a Yankee under Casey Stengel: "I still feel that the '42 Cardinal team was the best team I ever played on, better than all the Yankee teams. We had a young team, and it was a great ball club. We had good pitchers. We had *desire*."

STAN MUSIAL: "That was my first year. I was a rookie, fighting for a job. Who'd I have to beat out? Harry Walker. We had a great team, and I had a good season, and the way it ended up — getting in a World Series!

"Were we afraid of the Yanks? Well, they have an awesome reputation. We both trained down in St. Petersburg, and I was awed by Joe DiMaggio,

Charlie Keller, Tommy Henrich, Bill Dickey, Red Ruffing, Chandler. They had a good team, a darned good team. It was a *great* team. But we beat 'em in a city series down in St. Petersburg, so, you know, we got to know the Yanks. We had *our* club, too, and we were the younger team. Kurowski was new and I was new and Beazley was new. Then we had some veterans — Moore and Slaughter, Walker and Mort Cooper, Max Lanier. It was a good combination.

"The Cardinals had a great defensive club. Marion was a great shortstop, and we had Jimmy Brown at second and Johnny Hopp at first, and Slaughter and Moore and I — we were probably one of the fastest outfields I've seen. The Cardinals had a great spirit, a spirit about not knowing when to lose, and we *beat* the Yanks in that Series.

"In the second game, I hit a ball through the middle and drove in the winning run. That evened up the Series, and we went to New York. Left field is so huge in Yankee Stadium! It's one of the toughest fields I ever had to play. It's hard to feel comfortable in left field, because of the shadows. It's very deceiving applying the distance in Yankee Stadium. I couldn't pick up the ball from the bat.

"Gordon's drive? It was a line drive, but it kept lofting high, so it wasn't too hard to pick up. I was coming back on the ball, and I made a jumping catch. It probably would have been a home run.

"I think we upset the Yankee players and Joe McCarthy [the Yankee manager] during that Series. We were daring. We were taking extra chances, running from first to third on their good outfield. They were expecting to beat us. They had a confident club, a veteran club, and I think we upset McCarthy. For instance, he asked

Stan Musial was just a rookie when he and the speedy young Cards took the '42 World Series in four straight games. ST. LOUIS CARDINALS

the umpire to kick our clubhouse boy, Butch Yatkeman, off the bench. McCarthy wasn't concentrating on the games as such, and we were running wild.

"Nobody expected us to win four games in a row. I didn't expect to win four straight. I left my wife in St. Louis, thinking we were going to come back to play more World Series games in St. Louis. It didn't turn out that way. Who would ever expect that we'd beat the great New York team four in a row? I was happy. It's forty years

69

Mike (Mollie) Milosevich, immortal Yankee shortstop.
GEORGE BRACE

Bill (Goober) Zuber, Yankee pitching ace. GEORGE BRACE

since that time, but I remember it like it was yesterday."

Hey, Yankee fans! Remember Monk Dubiel? Mike Garbark? Mollie Milosevich? Bill (Goober) Zuber?

These were truly lovable Yankees, the pin-striped culls of 1944. Gone to war, where they belonged, were DiMaggio, Keller, Henrich — enough; you know the names.

Even so, the Yankees were picked to win the pennant. After all, every team was weak. The military draft had plucked baseball clean.

With the exception, that is, of the St. Louis Browns, an impoverished, woebegone team that had never won a pennant. By necessity, the Browns had always stocked their club with flawed athletes of one kind or another. In 1944 the Browns found themselves with more 4-F players than any other team in baseball. They also signed an aging, brawling, alcoholic pitcher, Sig Jakucki, who had already served in the Army — from 1927 to 1931.

While the Browns were inventive, using two part-time players who worked in war factories, the Yanks were stodgy, refusing to make the same use of their best relief pitcher, Johnny Murphy. "Using part-timers would demean big-league ball," huffed the Yankee president, Edward G. Barrow. "It would give us a semi-pro tone."

The Browns insulted the Yankees to start the season, winning their first nine games to break a league record set by the Yankees in 1933. The Yankees and their sycophantic writers could not believe that the scruffy Brownies might win. When the Yanks swept St. Louis in a doubleheader May 21, the *New York Times* wrote an early epitaph for the poor Browns: "It is questionable if they ever will be the same after what happened to them yesterday."

Yet somehow, with four games to go, the Browns still had a chance. So did the Yankees. Detroit led the Browns by one game and the Yankees by three. The Tigers would finish the season against last-place Washington, while the Yankees closed with four games in St. Louis.

It was time for Yankee thunder, but the thunderers were gone. The Browns swept a doubleheader, 4 to 1 and 1 to 0, then shut out the Yanks again, 2 to 0. Jakucki was picked to start the final game, and his teammates begged him to

stay sober the night before. He did, although he loosened up with a few snorts before game-time. While the Senators beat the Tigers, Chet Laabs hit two home runs and Vern Stephens one as the Browns humiliated the Yankees, 5 to 2, to win their only pennant.

LUKE SEWELL, the Brownie manager: "The greatest play that I ever saw in baseball? George McQuinn made it on the last day of the season in 19 and 44. There were two out in the ninth and Oscar Grimes was at bat and he hit a pop fly, about fifty or seventy-five feet high and about ten feet outside of first base. McQuinn caught it and it was the greatest play I

Even the Browns have disproved the Yankees' invincibility. Here, Sig Jakucki (shirtless, center) celebrates with his teammates after beating the Yanks on the final day of the 1944 season to give this St. Louis team their only pennant of the twentieth century. The happy man in the pinstriped suit is Don Barnes, owner of the team. Jakucki and Barnes are shaking hands with Mike Kreevich; behind Kreevich, with fist upraised, is Vern (Junior) Stephens, who later starred for the Red Sox.

ever saw in baseball. It cinched the pennant for us.

"The Yankees should have won the pennant. They had the personnel. A better team? Oh, yes. But you see, McCarthy had a system of baseball. He just turned those big bats loose and let 'em go. Joe's theory was that if he could intimidate you early in the season he didn't have to worry too much. But those big bats weren't there. They were in the Army. He was still playing that same kind of baseball, as if he had DiMaggio, Keller, Henrich, Dickey. Any number of games, if he had dropped some sacrifices in and things of that sort he would have won them from you."

That Skinny Guy Named Ted

A bunch of the boys came back from the war in 1946;
The writers thought that pin-striped team would give the league its licks.
DiMag is back, they said with pride, and Keller and Henrich and Red,
And all the Boston Red Sox have is that skinny guy named Ted.
But out of the gate, in the April chill, the Red Sox came with a crash.
While New England cheered, the Boston team set out on a pennant dash.
They pulled way ahead, and they crushed the ball; it wasn't a one-man show,
They had Rudy York and Bobby Doerr and the good DiMaggio.
Pesky played short, and the team's success went like wine to your head,
And when games were close the bat that won them was swung by skinny Ted.

Did you ever buy a baseball team that had lost its final spark?
A team that had sold its very soul to the devils in New York?
A team that had Ruth and Ruffing and Mays and sold them for Yankee gold,
And now you own that corpse of a team, and its failures turn you old.
Your name is Yawkey, and the years are long, and you've tried everything but sin.
You bought Grove and Foxx and Cronin and Ferrell and still you couldn't win.
You'd win some games and lose some games, but never make your mark
Against those ugly pin-striped ogres from the city of New York.

But all of a sudden the tune has changed, and Dom is outhitting Joe.
You look down, and the Yanks look up, from seventeen games below.
When the grisly nightmares of seasons past drag you from your bed,
You read the standings in the *Boston Globe*, and the Red Sox are still ahead.

The season wears on, and still you wonder, and tremble and sweat with fear,
Can Ferriss and Hughson and Harris and Dobson keep pitching like this all year?
Can old Pinky Higgins stay on his feet? What if he dies in bed?
What, God help me, will *we* ever do if something happens to Ted?

But the pin-striped sluggards never challenge, never start to hit.
Greenberg pulls the Tigers up, but they don't scare you a bit.
At the season's end you've won the flag, and when the MVP is read
You burst with pride, because the man who won it is that skinny guy named Ted.

"That Skinny Guy Named Ted." BOSTON RED SOX

73

Lou Boudreau and Bob Feller, Yankee killers extraordinaire, and stars of the champion Cleveland Indians of 1948.

the Yankees came to town. A spotter was stationed behind the scoreboard, looking through to steal signs from the Yankee catcher. The spotter would put a black or white card in a certain slot to signal curve or fastball. Joe Gordon by then had been traded to Cleveland, and in a game late in the 1948 pennant race, with the count three and nothing, he homered off Yankee pitcher Joe Page on a curve ball — an unusual time to swing, much less to detect a curve. Yankee players erupted from their dugout, screaming and pointing at the scoreboard. The Indians professed innocence.

Al Lopez managed the Indian champions of 1954 and the White Sox winners of 1959. Excepting 1954, his teams finished second to the Yankees for eight straight years — the Indians from 1951 through 1956, the White Sox from 1957.

LOPEZ, on 1954: "We had by far the best pitching staff I ever saw on any ball club. We had Bob Lemon, Bob Feller, Mike Garcia and Early Wynn, great pitchers, and then we came up with two kids by the name of Narleski and Mossi, and we had Hal Newhouser, who helped us quite a lot in the bullpen.

"We were about five or five-and-a-half games in front going down the stretch in September and we had a doubleheader with the Yankees on a Sunday, in Cleveland. They came in just for that doubleheader. We had the biggest crowd ever in Cleveland — 86,000 people. Lemon and Wynn both pitched beautiful games, and we beat 'em. That kind of clinched the pennant. The Yankees won 103 games that year, more games than any other Yankee team under Casey Stengel. But we happened to win 111."

It is awful, truly awful, that the Yankees lost only three pennant races in the eighteen seasons from 1947 through 1964. It is simple justice that they lost two of them to teams owned by Bill Veeck, a cheerful man utterly lacking in the pomposity so prized by the Yankees. The starchy Yankee management loathed Veeck, insulted him, and at one point drove him out of baseball. He loathed them back, needled them, squirmed back into baseball, and snatched another pennant from the Yankees.

74   Veeck's championship teams were the Cleveland Indians of 1948 and the Chicago White Sox of 1959. He was not one to miss an opportunity. In Cleveland he had movable outfield fences installed and moved them back all the way when

Your turn, Dodger fans. Let's revel in the 1955 World Series, the one that broke Brooklyn's miserable skein of seven straight lost Series, the last five of them to the hated Yankees. This was the Series of Johnny Podres's heroic pitching and of Sandy Amoros's memorable catch of Yogi Berra's drive in the seventh game.

PEE WEE REESE, the veteran Dodger shortstop: "I had played in the Series in '41, '47, '49, '52 and '53, all against the Yankees. They kept beating us every year. They would be ready for the Series; they would go to the National League and pick up an Enos Slaughter, a Johnny Hopp, Johnny Sain, Johnny Mize. Our ball club would never do that. Did the Yankees have more money? Well, the Dodgers should have had money. We drew over a million people, and they didn't pay us that much.

"By '55, I'm beginning to think, 'Am I ever going to be on a world's championship ball club?' We'd start thinking, 'What's going to happen now for us to lose?'

"We lost two games in a row, and then we came back and won three in a row. I can remember being on Ed Sullivan's show with some of the Yankees and some of the Dodgers. Whitey Ford was going to pitch the sixth game, and he said, 'I'll tell you one thing. There will be a seventh game.' And he was right. So now they won the sixth game and tied it up, and I thought, 'Well, hell, here we go. We lose two in Yankee Stadium, we win three in Ebbets Field. Then we go back to Yankee Stadium, they win the sixth game, and it looks like they'll win the seventh.'

"But thank heavens we had a young kid by the name of Johnny Podres who just pitched a whale of a ballgame.

"We almost lost that seventh game. Jim Gilliam was playing left field. Alston made the defensive change. He got Gilliam in at second base and moved Amoros out there in left. Billy Martin was on second and Gil McDougald was on first, and then came that ball Yogi hit.

"I don't think Sandy would have had to run that far if I had taken a look at him. He was over

Pee Wee Reese helped lead the Brooklyn Dodgers to vengeance in 1955.

75

in left-center, and Yogi did not pull lefthanders that much. Yogi hit the ball right down the left-field line. I thought it was gonna be in there — a double at least. I went out for the relay, down the line, and saw that McDougald had already rounded second. He thought the ball was in there. So I knew where McDougald was. I knew I'd have a shot at him.

"It's a good thing Sandy was lefthanded, because he was running right into the stands, his right arm out. I'm out in left field, say sixty or eighty feet down the left-field line. Sandy made a super play. He hit me with the throw. Did he know what McDougald was doing? Hell, no. The one thing on his mind was to get to that ball.

"Sandy relayed the ball to me, on the fly, with something on it. I didn't have to look around. I knew what I was going to do with the ball. The play was right in front of McDougald. He had to retrace his steps, touch the bag, and get back to first base. I knew if I went to first base instantly I had a chance to double him up. And I did. By how much? By a *hair*. Did that win it for us? Well, it sure as hell helped.

"We're down to the last out. Here's a man who's been in all these Series — I'm talking about myself — always wanting to be on a world championship team. I wasn't exactly out there saying, 'Hey, man, hit the ball to me. I want to make the last out.' No, I didn't have that feeling at all. I didn't want to screw this up. Elston Howard was up. We had gone over Howard, and he pulled the ball. Podres being a lefthander, he'd probably be a little more out in front of it. So I did shade him a few steps toward third, and it made the play a little bit easier. But it was hit in the hole. Some

said my throw was in the dirt and Hodges had to pick it up, but it wasn't. I just threw it out there so he could stretch out all the way.

"Afterwards, everybody reacted differently. I'm kind of low-key anyway. I wasn't exactly running around, jumping up and down and hollering, pouring champagne on everyone. I went over and sat down in front of my locker and just thought about this. We'd finally won a world championship. It's the highlight of my career. It really is. Finally winning the World Series, and finally beating the Yankees. I don't think I would have got as much kick out of it if we had played the White Sox or the Tigers or anybody else. Just to beat the Yankees. It really meant something."

WALTER ALSTON, the Dodger manager: "The thing that made me most proud of Amoros was the fact that he kept running and running hard all the way. A lot of outfielders might have shied away from that fence a little bit, but he kept going until the last second. He could have hurt himself on that fence, but he reached over and caught the ball and turned around and quickly made an accurate relay.

"A jinx? I never gave it much thought. You know, that was my first World Series, and I was so intent on what I was going to do — what changes I might make, who they had coming off the bench, what pitching changes might still be made — that I didn't think about this being the Dodgers' first championship. But after the last out was made, and we had won the Series, maybe a half hour after it was over, I felt like I had been run over with a truck."

Roy Campanella was proud to be in Dodger blue against the pinstripes.

ROY CAMPANELLA, the Dodger catcher: "An underdog feeling? No *way*. We were proud. I played with the Dodgers ten years, and in those ten years we won the pennant five years, finished second four years, and third once. We lost to Bobby Thomson of the Giants on his home run with two outs in the ninth inning. We lost to the Phillies when Duke Snider singled to center field and the winning run was thrown out at the plate. That's two of them, and the other years we were only one or two games out of first place. In the Series, we often got to the seventh game, and then you either win or lose. Over ten years, what team could say that?

"This young man Podres had one of the best change-ups of any young man who ever came into the major leagues. Johnny Podres had a *tremendous* change-up. It made his fastball faster than what it actually looked to be. And he had a good curveball. I always felt that if you could keep the hitter off stride you could change up on any hitter. The Yankees had so many good left-handed hitters, and in the final game I'd say approximately half of Podres's pitches were change-ups. Yes, and he got away with it. As long as he was successful, I kept calling for it."

As a part-time player for the Milwaukee Braves in 1957, Nippy Jones had time to shine his shoes before the fourth game of the World Series. His black shoes gleaming, Jones stepped in as a pinch-hitter to open the bottom of the tenth inning, with the Braves trailing the Yankees 5 to 4. An inside curve was called a ball. Jones insisted that the pitch hit his foot, and when umpire Augie Donatelli demurred, the inventive Jones retrieved the ball and showed it to the umpire. See? Shoe polish! Donatelli matched the mark on the ball with the wax on Jones's shoes and sent him to first base. Johnny Logan doubled home the tying run, and Eddie Mathews followed with a game-winning homer. The Kiwi bird was siding with the good guys.

The Yankees have been praised for their wisdom in acquiring veteran Johnny Sain from the Braves in 1951, but those accounts neglect to mention that the Yankees gave the Braves $50,000 — and a rookie pitcher named Lew Burdette. Contrary to the stereotypical player who supposedly yearns to remain a Yankee forever, Burdette was delighted to leave. "I didn't much like the Yankees after I came up from the minors," Burdette recalls. "They didn't make you feel too good. They gave you a uniform about four sizes too large — made you look like you were going swimming or something. And no locker; a nail in the corner."

BURDETTE beat the Yankees three times in the 1957 World Series. All three were complete games, including a shutout in the finale. Burdette's toughest moment may have been in his very first inning of the Series, when Mantle hit a ball sharply up the middle. "Mantle's hit got me in the family jewels. I didn't know whether to forehand or backhand it, so I tried to backhand it, and it caught me in the groin. It smarted for quite a while, and you can't rub down there.

"I still have the book that we used on the Yankees — high and tight, low and away. That meant a fastball high and a curveball away, and I didn't have either of 'em, so I did it my own way. I had a sinker that tailed away from the left-handed hitters. A spitter? They thought I was loading it up, but it was a psychological thing. One spring I asked Burleigh Grimes, the old spitballer, to show me how to throw a spitter. He said, 'Hell, it won't do you any good. They'll just catch you and you'll get in trouble. I always got more batters out when they thought I was throwing it.' So that's what I did. I threw that sinker, and it got 'em to complaining when they went back to the bench."

Bill Mazeroski gave America reason to smile in 1960; his seventh-game, ninth-inning homer sealed the Yankees' fate.

78

The Cremation of the Yankees

There are strange things done 'neath the October sun by the men who play to win.
The Series trails have their thrilling tales that could make your blood run thin.
Those autumn lights have seen strange sights, but the strangest they ever did see
Was the Series played in 1960: Pittsburgh, four games to three.

Now the Yankee team seemed quite supreme, with Mantle and Berra and all.
Compared to the spindly Pirates, those Yanks stood strong and tall.
They had no mercy, those Yankee thugs, and they mauled for all to see.
They won ten to naught and twelve to zip and in one game, sixteen to three.

But in between, the Pittsburgh team did all a team could do.
Mazeroski won a game with a homer, and Elroy Face saved two.
And in the seventh game a pebble gained fame, when a grounder bounced like heck,
And that crazy ball off Virdon's bat hit Kubek in the neck.
Tony was silent, his golden voice preserved for future years,
And Hal Smith hit a three-run homer that drove ol' Case to tears.
But the Pirate pitching was all worn out, and in the ninth the Yanks scored two;
That tied the game, and the Yanks smelled fame, and the fans a Waterloo.

The Pirates were tired, but their spirits were fired, and they wanted to win that game
And trip the pretentious Yankees with their dreams of the Hall of Fame.
Well it didn't take long. Maz's hit was gone, over the leftfield fence,
And he danced around the bases in a scene of jubilance.
So the Pittsburgh team had fulfilled a dream, as sweet as the Liberty Bell,
And America smiled as Maz's homer condemned the Yankees to Hell.

Yankee Stadium, October 2, 1963: The first game of the World Series. Whitey Ford for the Yankees, Sandy Koufax for the Dodgers. The Yankee play-by-play:

First inning
Tony Kubek struck out.
Bobby Richardson struck out.
Tom Tresh took a called third strike.

Second inning
Mickey Mantle was called out on strikes.
Roger Maris struck out.
Elston Howard fouled out to the catcher.

Third inning
Joe Pepitone struck out.
Clete Boyer grounded out.
Ford fouled out.

Fourth inning
Kubek struck out.
Richardson struck out.
Tresh was called out on strikes.

The game's last batter, a forgotten pinstriper named Harry Bright, was Koufax's fifteenth strikeout victim, breaking the World Series record of fourteen — which, incidentally, had been set by Brooklyn's Carl Erskine against the Yankees in 1953.

Three games later, the Series was over. The Yankees had scored four runs and lost four straight games — two to Koufax, one to Don Drysdale, the other to that fellow Podres.

80

KOUFAX: "We'd gone over the Yankee hitters. I knew the hitters and their strengths. But a game plan is not some-

Sandy Koufax struck out a record fifteen batters in game one of the 1963 series; the Dodgers won four in a row. LOS ANGELES DODGERS

thing that really works in baseball. It's a reaction game. You work according to the situation. I had real good stuff the first few innings, and more than that I had really good control. I made the pitches I wanted to make. But I didn't think I had that great stuff, to have so many strikeouts. It really surprised me a little bit.

"It wasn't any kind of exceptional day. Just a ball game. It just happened to be a World Series. The Yanks didn't make it a special situation. There was just as much exhilaration in '65 beating the Twins."

Okay, Sandy. But *we* thought it was pretty special.

A year later, things were reversed. Playing the Cardinals, the Yankees won two of the first three games. They beat the St. Louis ace, Bob Gibson, and in the fourth game they knocked out Ray Sadecki in the first inning with three runs.

ROGER CRAIG was the Cardinal reliever: "Before the game, our manager, Johnny Keane, said, 'You get ready in the first inning. Sadecki's sometimes a little nervous.' Sure enough, I came in the game in the first inning. I pitched pretty well in relief. I pitched four and two-thirds innings, struck out eight men, and they got two hits.

"In the third I walked Mantle, and he got to second base. I'll never forget what happened next. It was a play without any signs, what we call a 'daylight play.' A pitcher looks at his shortstop. When he can see daylight between a base runner and his shortstop, and the shortstop's inside the

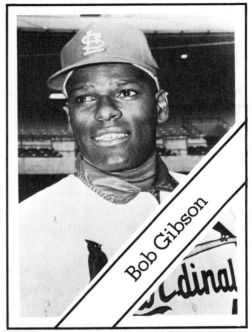

Bob Gibson. You'd look as contented as he does if you'd fanned thirty-one Yankees in the 1964 World Series.

baserunner, you know he can be beaten to the base. Our shortstop, Dick Groat, broke to the bag, and I threw it, and we picked him off.

"Then Ron Taylor came in, and he pitched four innings, too, without a hit. That was pretty good relief pitching. In eight and two-thirds innings we allowed two hits."

Broadcasters were filling air time during that Series by comparing the Yankee third baseman, Clete Boyer, with his brother, Ken, the Cardinal third baseman. Both were superb fielders. Clete

81

had hit .218 that season, with eight homers and fifty-two runs batted in. Ken had hit .295, with twenty-four homers and 119 runs batted in, enough to lead the league. Weighing these records with the usual Bronx impartiality, the broadcasting consensus seemed to be that both were swell players. But in the sixth inning of that fourth game, Ken proved to be sweller. He hit a grand-slam homer to win the game.

Gibson struck out thirteen in the fifth game and Tim McCarver homered in the tenth to win it. Two days later Gibson was back, striking out nine to bring his total for the Series to thirty-one. The Cardinals had beaten the Yankees for the third time in five Series, starting back in 1926.

Jim Kaat came up with the old Washington Senators in 1959 and moved with them to Minnesota, where he starred for the Twins. He was still pitching in 1982 and by then had experienced three generations of Yankee teams.

KAAT speaks about the Yankees' descent: "Nobody gave the Twins a real legitimate shot in '65. We had done well in '62 and '63, and then in '64 we fell off to seventh. I can remember in '65 even when we had a pretty comfortable lead — we had seven or eight games on Baltimore and Chicago, and the Yankees were maybe fourteen games out — still, everybody was figuring, 'Well, how many more do the Yankees have to lose before they're out?' Everybody had that kind of feeling, that once we got them eliminated the job would be a lot easier.

"The key game in our season was just before

Harmon Killebrew, whose flair for dramatic hitting keyed the Twins' pennant drive in 1965.

the All-Star break. The Yanks had beaten us the first game of a doubleheader, and then I got knocked out and we were down one run going into the last inning with two out, a man on, and Killebrew hitting. It was a very dramatic time. He fouled off a lot of pitches and then he hit a two-run homer that won the ball game. It was the difference in our splitting the series and keeping about a five-game lead versus going down to three games, and it would have been a real downer to lose a doubleheader just before the All-Star break. That was really a big lift for us.

"Did the Twins' pennant in '65 give the players a different feeling about the Yanks? I think it did. Once they lost, everybody finally had the feeling, 'Well, it's the end of the dynasty. They're not invincible.' Then the next year Baltimore got Frank Robinson. They had that big year, and it was a long time before the Yankees won.

"I don't think other teams have a feeling that they're so superior now as opposed to what they were in the '60s, prior to free agency. I mean, that was a real dynasty. They were head and shoulders above everybody else. They built their ball club from their own system and through an occasional trade. Now, it's just that their owner's in a position to — Hell, spend every conceivable dollar he can lay his hands on to put a winning ball club on the field.

"I don't root for the Yankees, because of George Steinbrenner. I feel bad when one of my good friends like Tommy John gets beat, but by the same token there's a satisfaction, because I can say, 'Well, they stuck it to George again.'

"I had kind of a personal thing. George was not honest with me in my dealings with him. George

Jim Kaat isn't the only player around who likes to see George's boys take their lumps. ST. LOUIS CARDINALS

had promised me a guaranteed contract shortly after the end of the '79 season, and he backed out of it. I had to go to spring training in 1980 and sort of prove myself again. Fortunately for me, I had a very productive spring training, and also Rudy May had an injury at the time, so they almost had to carry me. Also on the money angle, George reneged a little bit on what we had talked about. There are very few people in this game I have any personal bitter feelings toward, but he's one of 'em."

83

Who Remembers Dooley Womack?

A baseball reader endures a lot in the history of the game.
The books all start with Babe and Lou and remind you of their fame.
There were other teams, to be sure, they say, but let's forget about those,
And they never mention Dooley Womack, much less Roger Repoz.

They glory in the misty names of Gomez and Ruffing and Keller.
They tell you that DiMaggio was an extraordinary feller.
They echo these names like Greeks with their gods and tell how they vanquished their foes,
But they never write about Dooley Womack, much less Roger Repoz.

Mickey and Whitey come off in these books like a couple of cute little kittens,
And witty old Casey is the nice old man who had to keep track of their mittens.
Yankee wins are written about in the style of the Dead Sea Scrolls,
But the scriptures ignore Dooley Womack, and likewise Roger Repoz.

These books talk of eras and dynasties, which all belong to the Yanks,
But they leave out the one for which America gives thanks.
For eleven years the hated Yankees took it on the nose,
And their stars were turkeys like Dooley Womack and outfielder Roger Repoz.

Hark back to that age, from '65 through 1975
When the Orioles and the Oakland A's ate the Yanks alive.
When Jim Palmer was blazing the ball past Mick, and Frank Robby was smashing his blows,
And the batters feasted on Dooley Womack, and the pitchers on Roger Repoz.

But let's not forget those heroic Yanks, let the ages echo their names:
Ruben Amaro, Charley Smith — Mel Stottlemyre lost twenty games.
Horace Clarke, Jake Gibbs, Hal Reniff, Dick Howser, Gene Michael — his name ever glows
Alongside that of Dooley Womack, and his teammate Roger Repoz.

Let the organ play and the mist roll back from the Yankee Stadium shrine
Where the heroes of Yankee dynasties are adored like Father Divine.
There's Ruth and Gehrig, DiMag and Mick, and soon, if justice shows,
A noble bust of Dooley Womack and a statue of Roger Repoz.

WOMACK

REPOZ

Legend has it that the Yankees are the lightning rod that sparks interest in baseball, but during this glorious period no one seemed to miss the Yanks, not even in New York. The fans, in fact, began to desert Yankee Stadium even before the team collapsed. The favorites in New York were not the tiresome Yankees but the bumbling Mets, an expansion team that won friends while losing games — a refreshing mirror image of the Yankees, who aroused hatred with success. In 1964 the Yanks won the pennant and drew 1.3 million fans. The Mets finished last and drew 1.7 million.

Then, glory be, the Mets suddenly won a pennant in 1969 behind the superb pitching of Tom Seaver, Jerry Koosman, Tug McGraw, Gary Gentry and Nolan Ryan. Their manager, appropriately enough, was Gil Hodges, the former Dodger star. The Yanks finished fifth that season and drew barely a million fans. The Mets drew more than 2 million.

SEAVER, speaking during the 1982 spring training, recalls those days: "On any team you play for, there's a special relationship that the fans have with the players. It's different in every town. In New York they were very knowledgeable baseball fans, and they really appreciated hustle. They appreciated effort as much as they did excellence of performance. We were the darlings of the National League fans in New York. It was the old contingent of the Dodger and Giant fans; they were the people who gravitated to the Mets. We inherited the National League fans and the anti-Yankee fans — people who want to see somebody play other than the Yankees. Were there a lot of those? Sure. Still are.

Tom Seaver and the 1969 Mets provided New Yorkers with a real ball club to cheer. CINCINNATI REDS

Probably just as many as there are die-hard Yankee fans.

"We never thought of ourselves as relative to the Yankees, but that was probably on the fans' minds. Ownership is more attuned to that. It feeds their egos more than it should — much more than it should. Our owner, M. Donald Grant, used to get upset if we didn't have a good pitcher ready to pitch against the Yankees in the Mayor's Trophy Game. And you know Steinbrenner — he'd go nuts if the Mets would beat him.

"Do the Yanks have too great an advantage with all their money? I'm not so sure it's healthy for the game, but that's to presume that George Steinbrenner in all his wisdom is correct in his decisions. If they were to win every year it wouldn't be healthy for the game, but they just haven't devised a smart enough individual to be able to come up with that kind of superior ball club, no matter the money. They haven't won in 1982 yet, have they?"

By 1974 the Yankees had Chris Chambliss, Graig Nettles, Bobby Murcer, Lou Piniella, Thurman Munson and Roy White, among others, and late in the season they began a streak that threatened to end this serenely happy era of baseball. The Red Sox collapsed in September, and the Yankees pulled ahead. But streaking at an equal clip were the Orioles, with their superb defense — pitchers Jim Palmer, Ross Grimsley, Mike Cuellar and Dave McNally; infielders Brooks Robinson, Mark Belanger and Bobby Grich; center fielder Paul Blair.

J IM PALMER: "I can remember listening to a ball game when Boston had an eight-game lead on both the Yankees and us. Curt Gowdy said, 'Well, all the Red Sox have to do is win twenty-two out of their next forty-five games — go twenty-two and twenty-three — and the Orioles and Yankees will have to play .700 baseball.' Well, Boston lost eight games in a row, so that changed the numbers dramatically. In fact, they finished way back in third place.

"It was the first time I was in a close pennant race. It was very enjoyable because both teams were playing well. Every game was exciting. The whole month of September, it was a one-game advantage for either team. We went into New York having to win three in a row. McNally pitched one and Cuellar pitched one and I pitched one. Two were shutouts and in the third the Yanks might have gotten one run. In the last series of the season, we were playing Detroit and I remember listening as George Scott got a hit up the middle for Milwaukee."

Scott's hit beat the Yankees and clinched the pennant for Baltimore, but there was a story behind that hit — a typically Yankee story. According to accounts of the game, Scott's hit might have been caught had Murcer been at his usual outfield position. But Murcer was injured, and his replacement, Lou Piniella, couldn't get to the ball. A principal in the bizarre story behind Murcer's injury was Rick Dempsey, now the Oriole catcher but then a Yankee substitute, as was the other principal, Bill Sudakis.

D EMPSEY: "We had just finished a series in Cleveland, and we had a two-and-a-half- or three-hour layover in the airport on our way to Milwaukee. Some of the guys were in the airport bar getting a little sauced up. One of them was Bill Sudakis. On the plane, he started picking on somebody. It didn't matter who it was—just anybody who came close. I was sitting in the seat behind him with Thurman Munson, and he started on me saying things that were really off color — not the kind of things you say to somebody kidding around or joking around. There really wasn't much I could do at that time but just sit there and take it. It was a commercial flight. We were all sitting up front, and there were

Rick Dempsey, with manager Earl Weaver. Dempsey helped clinch the 1974 pennant for the Orioles, even though he was a substitute catcher for the Yankees at the time.
JERRY WACHTER, BALTIMORE ORIOLES

regular passengers in the back of the plane. One guy was a little alarmed at Bill for using profane language in front of his wife. So he stood up and said something to Bill, and Bill jumped all over him, saying, 'You better sit down before I knock you down.'

"He was getting pretty much out of hand, and a few guys were agitating him at the same time, like Thurman. He wasn't going to get in a fight with Thurman, because Thurman was one of the big boys on the club.

"They served lunch. They put my sandwich down in front of me and Bill turned around and grabbed my sandwich and opened it up and slammed it down on my tray. Then he took my fork and acted like he was going to stab me with my fork. I tried not to pay much attention, but I was getting a little nervous about it. He kept telling me what a tough guy he was back in Chicago and how he'd go out and kick the heck out of these guys, and he showed me all the scars on his knuckles. It was getting kind of ridiculous. But there was one serious note: He kept saying, 'Do you want to street-fight or do you want boxing gloves? Anything you want. Come on, I want to kick your rear end.'

"At that point it got pretty serious. I had to pick my time and my place. We were riding on the bus from the airport, and Cecil Upshaw, one of our pitchers, came up to me and said, 'Why don't you just relax and forget about it.' I said, 'Well, I can't forget about it at this point. He's pretty much embarrassed me in front of the whole club. I've got to pick my spot now to make my amends.'

"When we got on the bus, it just so happened that Sudsy [Sudakis] sat right across from me, and I got a little nervous. Pre-fight nerves, I guess. I suspected something was going to happen, one way or the other. My legs started shaking. Bill looked at me and he says, 'What's the matter, are you nervous?' I said, 'Aw, no, I'm not nervous.' My legs are going di-di-di-di-di-di-di-di. He kept saying, 'I'm gonna get you. I'm really gonna get you. Soon as we get to the hotel, I'm gonna beat the hell out of you.' So I said, 'Yeah, sure, Bill. Sure you are.' So I waited, and I was the first guy off the back of the bus. I went in the lobby of the Hotel Pfister. I figured, 'I got a choice now, whether I get my key and go on up to my room and forget all about it, or do I make my stand, right here, because I've got plenty of room.'

"So I stopped right there with my back to the guys getting off the bus, and I waited. Everybody walked in front of me and got their keys. I was kind of hoping that he'd come up and say something else, because then I knew I would snap. Bobby Murcer came up to me, and he said 'Come on, you better forget all about it. We're in a pennant race, we're tied with the Orioles now. You better forget all about it.' I didn't hear a word that he said. It came back to me later, but I wasn't listening at the time.

"So Bill walked up and he tapped me on the shoulder and he says, 'Well, kid, what's it going to be? Street fighting or boxing gloves?' I said, 'Neither.' Boom-boom-boom! And it was all over. I hit him three times and that was it. Sudakis went down, and his glasses flew over the cashier's counter. And then I commenced to hitting everybody else on the ball club, too. I just kind of went crazy. Anybody that came close to me, I just started slugging.

"As soon as I hit Bill, he lost his balance, and hit Bobby Murcer on his way down. Bobby grabbed me around the ankles. He was trying to keep me from fighting, but he had me around the legs, which really gave me more stability. Dave Pagan, my roommate, ran up to grab me, and I hit him and knocked him over a chair. Then Pat Dobson came up. I hit him. The last guy I hit was Walt Williams. Walt tried to knock me down like a fullback. He just came in and buried his head in my chest. But Bobby was getting up at that time, and he was pushing me forward, so he solidified my stand. I gave Walt Williams an uppercut and he fell across the couch in the lobby, and just totally crushed the couch and knocked a fixture off the wall.

"I must have hit at least five guys. At the end of the fight I fell half in this bar that the Pfister had and half out of the bar. Elston Howard grabbed me, and Thurman Munson had me around the neck, and Dobson had gotten back up and he grabbed me. I couldn't move a muscle in my body. They picked me up and sat me in a chair in the bar. Elston bought me a drink. My arms were shaking so much that I couldn't hold the glass in my hand. He poured the whiskey down my throat just to get me to calm down.

"Through all this, that's how Bobby Murcer got hurt. I must have stepped on his hand, and I broke his finger. Piniella went in to play the outfield against Milwaukee. It was a 2 – 2 ballgame with a man on second base and a fly ball to right field, and the ball fell in about a foot in front of Piniella's glove. It probably would have been caught by Murcer, and maybe the game would have turned out different. Who knows? But they blamed the whole thing on the fact that Murcer wasn't in the lineup."

Ah, to have been in Dempsey's shoes, to have lived the fantasy of destroying the Yankees from the inside — and to fondly look back on it as a Yankee-hating Oriole!

When the Yankees win there is always worshipful talk of a dynasty, and so there was in 1976, the first pennant year under George Steinbrenner and Billy Martin. Steinbrenner was building his kind of team, with only two players, Thurman Munson and Roy White, from the Yankee farm system. But the baseball dynasty of that age was already established. It was in Cincinnati, where the Big Red Machine had just won its fifth division championship and fourth pennant of the decade. The previous October, the Reds had beaten the Red Sox in a World Series still regarded as perhaps the most dramatic in history.

This confident Cincinnati team virtually spat in the Yankees' face. Pete Rose played a daringly close third base to keep Yankee speedster Mickey Rivers from bunting, and catcher Johnny Bench threw Rivers out on his first steal attempt. Bench hit .533 for the Series, including two home runs in the fourth and last game of the Reds' sweep. In a press conference after the Series, Cincinnati Manager Sparky Anderson was asked to compare Bench with the Yankees' Munson, who had hit .529 himself. Bench was not present, but Munson, a proud man, was. "Don't embarrass anyone by comparing him to Johnny Bench," the ebullient Anderson said.

ANDERSON, six years later: "I had never been in Yankee Stadium, and I have to admit that going into Yankee Stadium you think about all the people that passed through — Babe Ruth, Joe DiMaggio, Mickey Mantle, the great McCarthy, Miller Huggins. It gives you a great awe, and all our players felt it when they went out on the field. It was very impressive. But I knew that if anybody beat us, they would have to do everything right. I was not concerned that we wouldn't win. We had just beat Philadelphia three straight in the playoffs, and I wanted to see us make it seven straight. I thought this club was that good. Winning seven straight in the playoffs and World Series, it would be judged as one of the great teams. I knew that if it wasn't one of the great teams ever, then them other teams — the '27 Yankees, some of those other clubs — man, they must have *really* been good. Because this was as good a club as I have ever seen put together."

BENCH: "I grew up in Oklahoma, and Mantle was from Oklahoma. I was a huge fan of his and the entire Yankee team. In those days there were only two teams that won, the Dodgers and the Yankees. Because Mantle was from Oklahoma, I really fell in love with him. Mantle was so great. That was what I aspired to be.

"Were we awed by the Yanks in '76? Not at all. We were the team to beat. We were the '75 world champions, we had had a great season, and we went through the playoffs in three games. I don't think we felt that the Yankees or anybody else was as good a team as we were. The Yankees knew that we were world champions, and here we were back again. It seemed like they were tight. We were a ball club with *so* much confidence.

"I had not had a good year in '76. I had a

Johnny Bench and the Big Red Machine stomped all over the Yankees in the '76 Series. CINCINNATI REDS

tremendous amount of muscle spasms in my back. I sort of got my stroke going into the playoffs, and I was just hoping for some good games to counteract a bad season. So the Series for me was a personal enjoyment — just unbelievable. Throwing Rivers out, and getting him fairly easily the first time. The triple I got off [Doyle] Alexander in the first game. And I got a couple of hits off Catfish in the second game. Do I remember the pitches I hit for homers in the last game? Fastball by Figueroa, up and in. Slider off Tidrow. You don't forget too much about a World

91

Series. You shouldn't. Sometimes it's nice to go back and watch the replays."

TONY PEREZ, the Reds' first baseman: "We had a great team, and we were very confident we could beat the Yankees. We never counted on beating them four straight, but we knew we could beat them in five or six games. We came out in four because we really played much better than we thought we could. You got the designated hitter that Series, so Dan Driessen was allowed to play. He had a great Series. I had a good Series. Everybody had a good Series. We depended more on offense than pitching, but the pitching did great.

"In one game they almost beat us. They had men in scoring position, and Thurman Munson hit a line drive over my head. I jumped, and I was lucky. I don't know how I jumped *that* far, but I got the ball and I threw the man out at second, and we made a double play to get out of that inning. In the second game, I came up with the bases loaded in the ninth inning against Catfish Hunter. He was tough. He went after you, and his ball really took off. The only way he could stop me was with a fastball. I was ready for it. He threw me a fastball on the first pitch, and I got a base hit to win that game.

"That was my first time in Yankee Stadium, and it really was exciting for me. I grew up in Cuba. My father was a Yankee fan. I liked the Brooklyn Dodgers. The Yankees always beat them, so I got to hate the Yankees a little bit. I was against the Yankees most of the time. Then I play in Yankee Stadium, and we beat them in four straight, and that was great. I was so happy."

Tony Perez grew up hating the Yankees a little bit.
BOSTON RED SOX

After the Series, the Yankee players — by far the best-paid in baseball — voted against giving any share of their World Series money to their batboys. The Reds voted their batboys $6,591 each. Chastened, the Yankees reached to the depths of their generous souls, and gave their batboys a whole $100.

By 1979 the Yankees had won three straight pennants, and the sports journalism establishment was so entranced with their oafish owner, angry manager and childishly petulant players that the 1979 pennant race slipped by almost unnoticed. The Baltimore Orioles won it with a superbly balanced team, skillfully managed by Earl Weaver. The Yankees never contended and barely finished fourth, but the networks continued to put them on nationwide television week after week. "Do you take the Orioles seriously?" a writer asked Reggie Jackson midway in the season when Baltimore was well out front. "I take them seriously as death," Jackson replied.

When, finally, a network grudgingly gave the fans a peek at the team with the best record in baseball, its analyst looked upon them as strangers, and was hard put to explain their success. "They're not a home-run hitting club," he said. In fact, the Orioles hit 181 home runs, 31 more than the Yankees.

RICK DEMPSEY, the Oriole catcher: "The fact that Steinbrenner has gone out and bought everything upsets everybody, because everybody else feels like they don't have much of a chance against the almighty dollar — and George has so many of 'em. But that's not necessarily true. In 1979 we put everything together and we blew them out. We beat the Yankees by thirteen-and-a-half ball games, so it's not really money that can put you in first place. You have to have a lot of quality players, players who are willing to play together, and we did that in '79.

"We played the Yankees eight games late in the year, right about the time we were getting close to wrapping it up, and we beat 'em five out of eight.

It was publicized in the newspapers that Baltimore was more than anxious to beat the Yankees to prove to George Steinbrenner that he didn't have the best team money could buy. There's always an incentive to beat the Yankees because we don't have the big names in baseball — the Reggie Jacksons and Graig Nettles and Willie Randolphs and Bucky Dents. George just goes out and gets anybody who's a good hitter that's on the free-agent market. He doesn't care what he pays. He just goes out and buys 'em. And then when he does have trouble — this guy complaining because he doesn't have as much money in his contract as another player does — that just adds to our incentive.

We're sitting over here with eight or nine guys making less that $100,000, and we think, 'Now what the heck is wrong with these guys? What more can George give them to make 'em happy? Let's just beat the heck out of 'em!' "

JIM PALMER has beaten the Yankees more than any other active pitcher — twenty-eight times through 1982. "I spent the first nine years of my life in New York, and I idolized the Yankees. I remember reading the headlines in the old *Daily Mirror*: YANKEES SWEEP 2. The most dramatic year of my life was 1954 when they won 103 games and still lost to Cleveland. We moved out west, and my fondest memory of going to school in Beverly Hills was between history and geography, listening to the radio to see who was winning the World Series between the Dodgers and Yankees back in '55 and '56. In '57 I didn't like the Milwaukee Braves very well, because they were beating the Yankees.

"When I was in high school, out in Scottsdale, the Yankees scouted me and came and talked to my parents. The guy said, 'We want to sign your son.' But the Yankees never got back to them, and I got some good offers from other ball clubs and ended up signing with the Orioles. My first year in organized ball, 1964, the Orioles finished two games behind. The Yankees won, and I rooted for the Yankees the whole year. They were my favorite team. I didn't care about the Orioles.

"My first victory in the big leagues, back in 1965, I came in in relief and hit a home run off Jim Bouton over the right-center field fence in Baltimore and won the game. Later in the season I came in on Labor Day, second game of a double-header. Frank Bertaina started the game for us and got hit on the hand with a line drive. He left runners on first and second. We were trailing 2 – 0, and Horace Clarke hit a broken-bat squibber between third and short that Aparicio caught, and he held it to bases loaded, nobody out. I struck out Mantle, Maris and Howard on about ten fastballs with the bases loaded, in Yankee Stadium. I pitched, I think, five innings, struck out ten. Andy Etchebarren hit a three-run inside-the-park home run up the gap in left-center, and Curt Blefary hit a two-runner in the upper deck in right field, and Stu Miller came in and finished the game. We won 5 to 2. It was the first time Hank Bauer, our manager, ever really said anything to me. He had played so many great years for the Yankees, and he liked to beat the Yankees so much. 'Nice going, kid,' he said.

"Those were the biggest games I've ever played. I have fond memories. I struck Mantle out about the first five or six times that he ever faced me. Then I had a 2 – 0 lead in about the seventh inning in New York in 1966, and he came up, and he choked up on the bat. Etchebarren, our catcher, said, 'Mickey, you're choking up!' He said, 'Yeah, this kid throws too hard.' I had a 2 – 0 lead, nobody on, and I went two balls, no strikes, and I kind of took a little bit off the fastball, and he *hit it.* There used to be a football spotting box about the third deck right above the old Yankee bullpen in right-center field, and he hit a crisp line drive off that. The ball was hit *rather hard.*

"Tradition? There's no Yankee tradition any more, as far as I'm concerned. George can say that you have to be proud to wear the pinstripes, but the pinstripe does not stand for what it used to. It used to be that despite all the rumors about having a farm club in Kansas City and things like that, they built through more old-type values, building, having a good farm system, having good players. Now you want to beat the Yankees because of what they stand for. Really, it's trying to say to yourself, 'Hey, can the have-nots beat the haves?' The Orioles have always developed from within. It's like being a little corporation and fighting AT&T or General Motors. It's difficult to do, but through hard work and teamwork — clichés, but it's true — we, the Orioles, have the best record in baseball. The Yankees used to be synonymous with winning. Now they're synonymous with big bucks."

Jim Palmer grew up as a Yankee fan, but he struck out Mantle the first half-dozen times they met and has since helped the Orioles achieve the best record in baseball. JERRY WACHTER, BALTIMORE ORIOLES

Brett Against Gossage

There are times when a whole season can be seen in a single day,
When months of excitement and runs and hits are distilled in a single play,
When it's just the right game, on just the right day, with just the right man at bat,
And just the right pitcher is out on the mound, tugging at his hat.

The good team was Kansas City, a bridesmaid for too many years,
Against the wicked New York Yankees, loathed for their pouts and their tears.
The year was 1980, in playoff game Number Three,
The Yankees were trailing two games to none, but the Royals weren't home free.

They were haunted with memories of failure, they knew that they still could fall,
And out on the mound stood big Goose Gossage, crude and mean and tall.
The Yankees were leading with two men out and Royals on first and third,
And the batter for Kansas City was the man the fans preferred.

His name was Brett, he played third base, and he hit .390 that year,
And he mouthed his chaw, and eyed the Goose, and tapped the plate without fear.
Gossage pitched and Brett swung, and Gossage craned his neck,
And Brett's long drive brought the pennant home as it fell in the upper deck.

George Brett made the Goose lay an egg.
KANSAS CITY ROYALS

The 1981 World Series was satisfying not only because the Dodgers won it, but because the Yankees did so much to *lose* it. George Steinbrenner's most expensive baubles — Dave Winfield, Reggie Jackson, Tommy John — made embarrassing mistakes, and the Dodgers, a largely home-grown team, capitalized on them, displaying a characteristic that the Yankees considered their own. Was this a Yankee team without character, as critics of Steinbrenner and his spoiled players have claimed? Who knows, but consider these delightful highlights:

• Leading two games to none, the Yankees threatened in the eighth inning of the third game against rookie Fernando Valenzuela, who, according to his manager, Tom LaSorda, "had his worst stuff of the year." Bobby Murcer, an old Yankee bought back by Steinbrenner to help in just such moments, displayed a typical Yankee shortcoming: He couldn't bunt. Instead of a roller, he bunted a soft line drive which Ron Cey alertly caught and converted into a double play. The Dodgers won, 5 to 4, with Valenzuela going the distance.

• Trailing 6 to 3 in the sixth inning of the fourth game, the Dodgers pulled to within one on a two-run homer by pinch-hitter Jay Johnstone. Davey Lopes followed with an easy fly to short right field. We watched, millions of us, with unbelieving joy, as the ball bounced off Reggie Jackson's chest. Lopes made it to second, stole third, and scored on Bill Russell's single, tying the game. That's not all. In the Dodger seventh, Dusty Baker singled and Rick Monday's liner to short center was muffed by Bobby Brown, who was playing only because he was a Steinbrenner favorite. Peal of thunder, roll of drums. Did John pitch his way into the history books? Nope; he yielded a sacrifice fly, a bunt, and a single by Lopes that drove in the winning run. The score was 8 to 7, Los Angeles. The Dodgers had tied the Series while resting their best pitchers for the final games.

• With Ron Guidry pitching superbly in the fifth game, the Yankees blew three scoring opportunities, much to the credit of Dodger pitcher Jerry Reuss. In the second, the Yankees scored a run and had two men on with no outs. Reuss stranded both runners. In the third, the Yanks had two on with one out and failed to score. In the fourth, they loaded the bases with

97

one out, but did not score. In the seventh, Guerrero and Steve Yeager hit sudden, back-to-back home runs for a 2 to 1 Dodger victory.

• There were many glorious sights in the sixth and final game, won by Los Angeles 9 to 2, but perhaps the most gratifying was contributed by Dave Winfield, the most grotesquely overpaid Yankee of all. With two out in the Yankee fifth and Willie Randolph on second base, Winfield popped up — and fell down doing it. This clumsy failure symbolized Winfield's inept Series performance; he got one single in twenty-two times up, and then had the presumption to stop play so he could retrieve the ball for a souvenir.

STEVE GARVEY, the Dodger star first baseman, had played in three previous World Series and lost them all, the last two to the Yankees. Garvey, who hit .417 to help the Dodgers win the '81 Series, revels in the memory: "It was a chance for us to get back and beat them, to redeem ourselves. We were looking forward to it. After starting out by losing the first two games, people were saying, 'Here we go again.' But we had a different feeling. We were getting back to our park, to our hometown fans. We knew we'd win at least two out of three in Los Angeles. And we won four straight. The pivotal game was the fifth one — beating Guidry when he pitched so well.

"Was it more satisfying to beat the Yankees than some other teams? Yeah, because we had lost that previous World Series to the Yankees. Not only winning the world championship and beating them, but by beating them at Yankee Stadium that last game we kind of dispelled a lot of philosophizing about us not being able to win in New York.

"The fans are more aggressive there. It's a different environment that they live in. The Dodger fans are very good, and they can be very loud, but they aren't as aggressive toward the other team. Are the Yankee fans a menace? Well, they are going to try to help their team any way they can.

"Compare a homegrown team like ours to the Yankees? To see somebody start out, a fresh young prospect, become a major leaguer and then a star — it's a nice, warm feeling. Whereas if you acquire people through trades or free agency it's not quite the same emotionally. Ultimately, a young team that develops into a champion is more satisfying. But the end justifies the means. We're an easy-going, public-relations-oriented team and we don't have as many controversies as the Yankees. You would probably be right in saying that more times than not, the Yankees would be hated.

"Yes, we'd like to play them again. It's the classic World Series. When the Dodgers play the Yankees it captures the interest of the rest of the world."

Steve Garvey found extra satisfaction in beating the Yankees at Yankee Stadium to win the 1981 World Series. LOS ANGELES DODGERS

In 1982, the Yankees captured the interest and pleasure of the rest of the world by falling deep into the second division and playing as if in parody of their owner's pompous claims and foolish strategies. In defeat as in victory, Yankee players matched Steinbrenner, petty remark for petty remark, until by season's end the list of players either traded or begging to go stretched from Ken Griffey's not-so-fleet feet to Goose Gossage's angry Fu Manchu.

A child could have told Steinbrenner that Reggie Jackson was the most valuable player on his team, in spirit and in deed. But Jackson, of all people, was cast adrift by Steinbrenner in favor of Griffey and Dave Collins, who were supposed to transform the Yankees into a running team. Critics questioned the change, but Steinbrenner knew he was right. "I'm sick and tired of hearing that this team doesn't have power," he said as the season began. "We have power and we have speed and we have everything that we should need to win. We put a lot of thought [sic] into planning this team and I feel that this is the most balanced team we've had in the ten years I've been here. If we're not really awesome, really exciting, I'll be surprised and disappointed."

For power, Steinbrenner picked up Butch Hobson and John Mayberry, both of whom were clearly over the hill. He over-fortified the Yankees at shortstop, where Roy Smalley replaced Bucky Dent, and at catcher, where Butch Wynegar took the place of Rick Cerone, at the cost of Ron Davis, who could not be spared from a pitching staff that already was perilously thin.

As the team's failures mounted, Steinbrenner shuffled managers and coaches like Hitler shuffled generals; *somebody* had to take the blame. His attempts to inspire the team drew ridicule from his own players, and the events of the season immortalized the Yankee owner as a buffoon — an improvement on his previous reputation.

On September 9, 1982, Steinbrenner issued this statement: "Other people may not think that we're battling for the pennant anymore, but we are and we are a proud team and we're not out of it until the last dog is dead." Yankee pitcher Rudy May responded: "The last dog? Which one of us is he talking about now?"

Responding to their owner's call, the Yankees charged off to Baltimore and Milwaukee, where the Eastern Division race was being waged. The Orioles beat the Yankees five in a row, winning three of the games behind rookie pitchers. The Brewers beat the Yankees three in a row, out-scoring them thirty-four to five. As Yankee Manager Clyde King put it, "We got eliminated in a big way."

Stout-Hearted George

Give me some men who are fleet-footed men
Who will win for the man they abhor
Just start me with Ken who can steal maybe ten
And Reggie can walk out the door.

Older and older, and colder and colder
Nettles is over the hill
But Wynegar and Smalley, Erickson and Rawley
Will give Yankee fans such a thrill!

I built this team, it's a manager's dream
But Lem was too nice to be tough
I brought Michael in, and his managing sin
Was his failure to win, so enough!

Davis and John wanted out so they're gone
And I traded our youngsters away
But wait 'til next year when the league shakes with fear
And Stout-Hearted George has his day.

CHAPTER NINE

Quotes to Make You Gloat

"Oh, Butch, you're not going to have to go to that animal farm, are you?"
> — Butch Wynegar's mother on hearing that her son, the Minnesota Twins' catcher, had been traded to the Yankees in May 1982

"If you want to get off this team, you have to take a number."
> — Dave Revering, shortly before his number came up in 1981; he was traded to Toronto

"It was just a big, unanimous thing that grew until it filled the park."
> — George Steinbrenner on the spontaneous "Steinbrenner sucks!" chant at Yankee Stadium

"It's about the only fun time I had in the game."
> — Ron Guidry, Yankee pitcher, on the same chant

"I've always said that if you wait and keep your mouth shut, things will come around right."
> — George Steinbrenner

"Lem will get the whole season, win or lose."
> — Steinbrenner in December 1981, announcing Bob Lemon's appointment as Yankee manager for 1982

"After what happened with Lem, I know people won't believe this but Stick is going to be the manager all year — and longer."

— Steinbrenner on April 25, 1982, announcing the dismissal of Lemon and the appointment of Gene Michael as Yankee manager

"Sometimes I wish you could let go of a lot of players instead of the manager. But the way baseball is structured, you can't do that. We have an awful lot of players who think they're a lot better than they really are."

— Steinbrenner on August 4, 1982, announcing the dismissal of Michael and the appointment of Clyde King as Yankee manager

"I want out. I'm sick of everything that goes on around here. I'm sick of all the negative stuff and you can take that upstairs to the fat man and tell him I said it."

— Goose Gossage on August 16, 1982. Steinbrenner responded that he wasn't so fat.

"A visit with the Yankees in spring training is not very different from turning up on a Caribbean island to marvel at the banking facilities."

— Vic Ziegel in *New York* magazine

"The Yankees can be had."

— Al Lopez, who had them twice, as manager of the Cleveland Indians in 1954 and of the Chicago White Sox in 1959

"They asked me to take it for a year and see if I liked it. Sometimes I did and sometimes I didn't."

— Yogi Berra, who managed the Yankees one season, won the pennant, and was fired

"I'm closer to him than any other owner I've ever had. I've gone out with him, and he's fun to be with."

— Billy Martin in 1977 on his friend, George Steinbrenner

"I don't expect there'll be any changes until tomorrow."

— Bob Lemon after the Yankees lost the 1981 World Series. Actually, Lemon wasn't fired until the following spring.

"Kid, you're too small. You ought to go out and shine shoes."

> — Casey Stengel, then manager of the Dodgers, to a youngster named Phil Rizzuto at a Dodger tryout camp

"I suppose you were in the war."

> — Babe Ruth to Marshall Foch, French hero of World War I

"He treats fans with contempt and sportswriters even worse."

> — Murray Chass, writing about Graig Nettles in *The Yankees* (Random House, 1979)

"I don't want to dilute my impact."

> — Dave Winfield, Yankee outfielder, explaining why he hired a public relations firm

"I know I'll perform well...I'll put some numbers on the board one way or another, and make some defensive plays. People who know my abilities envision me as [Series] MVP."

> — Dave Winfield before the 1981 World Series. The numbers he put on the board were one for twenty-two.

"I want the Dodgers back in New York, back in the Bronx."

> — George Steinbrenner after the Dodgers won the fifth game of the 1981 World Series. Back in the Bronx, the Dodgers won the sixth and final game, 9 to 2.

"I cannot believe this."

> — Tommy John in the Yankee dugout after he was lifted for a pinchhitter in the fourth inning of the final game of the 1981 World Series, with the score tied 1 to 1.

"I want to sincerely apologize to the people of New York and to fans of the New York Yankees everywhere for the performance of the Yankee team in the World Series. I also want to assure you that we will be at work immediately to prepare for 1982."

> — George Steinbrenner, in a press release

"When the Yankees go out for dinner, they reserve twenty-five tables for one."

— An anonymous seer, quoted in *Sports Illustrated*

"The more we lose, the more Steinbrenner will fly in. And the more he flies, the better the chance there will be a plane crash."

— Dock Ellis, then a Yankee pitcher, in spring training of 1978, as quoted in *The Bronx Zoo*, by Sparky Lyle and Peter Golenbock

"The Yankees, too, are a family. A family like the Macbeths, the Borgias, and the Bordens of Fall River, Massachusetts."

— Ron Fimrite in *Sports Illustrated*, comparing the Yankees to the Dodgers

"The two of them deserve each other. One's a born liar; the other's convicted."

— Billy Martin, then — but not for long — the Yankee manager, on Reggie Jackson and George Steinbrenner

"We were just so happy to be in the World Series that we forgot what to do until it was too late."

— An anonymous Yankee after his team was swept by Cincinnati in the 1976 World Series

"You know, this team…it all flows from me. I've got to keep it going. I'm the straw that stirs the drink…Munson thinks he can be the straw that stirs the drink, but he can only stir it bad…The rest of the guys should know that I don't feel that far above them…I mean, nobody can turn people on like I can, or do for a club the thing I can do, but we are still athletes, we're all still ballplayers."

— Reggie Jackson in the famous June, 1977 *Sport Magazine* interview that so endeared him to his Yankee teammates

"The magnitude of me, the magnitude of the instance, the magnitude of New York. It's uncomfortable, it's miserable. It's uncomfortable being me, it's uncomfortable being recognized constantly, it's uncomfortable being considered something I'm not, an idol or a monster, something hated or loved."

> — Reggie Jackson, after being asked what he thought about during his suspension in 1978

"It is tough."

> — Reggie Jackson, reflecting on his career to a *Rolling Stone* reporter as Jackson lounged in the arms of a lovely blonde in a swank Miami club

"I don't mind being called a prick or a cocksucker or things like that. I expect that. But lay off the personal stuff."

> — Babe Ruth to members of the New York Giants, in the Giants' clubhouse, after the third game of the 1922 World Series. The Giants rode Ruth mercilessly during the Series, which the Giants swept.

"Fielding — He can't stop quickly and throw hard. You can take the extra base on him if he's in motion away from line of throw. He won't throw on questionable plays and I would challenge him even though he threw a man or so out.

Speed — He can't run and he won't bunt.

Hitting vs. righthanded pitcher — His reflexes are very slow and he can't pull a good fastball at all. The fastball is better thrown high, but that is not too important as long as it is fast. Throw him nothing but good fastballs and fast curveballs. Don't slow up on him.

Hitting vs. lefthanded pitcher — Will pull lefthand pitcher a little more than righthand pitcher. Pitch him the same. Don't slow up on him. He will go for a bad pitch once in a while with two strikes."

> The Brooklyn Dodgers' scouting report on Joe DiMaggio for the 1951 World Series

106

"She's a plain kid. She'd give up the business if I asked her. She'd quit the movies in a minute."

> — Joe DiMaggio on his bride, Marilyn Monroe, who instead quit the marriage

"What the hell is going on here?"
    — Joe DiMaggio, watching Marilyn's skirt being blown high during filming
    of a famous scene of *The Seven Year Itch*

"My life in Hollywood was dull."
    — Joe DiMaggio

"Some people are leaders and some are followers. I'm a follower."
> — Mickey Mantle on his role in the great Copacabana nightclub fight of 1957. The Yankee management decided that Billy Martin was the leader and traded him to Kansas City.

YANKEES TRAINING ON SCOTCH
> — Headline in a New York newspaper during spring training, 1922.

MAN BITES DOG
> — Headline in a Boston newspaper when the Red Sox bought a player from the Yankees in 1934.

"Everyone expects the Yankees to win the pennant, and so do I."
> — Johnny Keane when hired as Yankee manager before the 1965 season. The Yanks finished sixth.

"We're more determined than last year."
> — Yankee catcher Elston Howard before the 1966 season. The Yanks finished last.

"We are out to win ball games. We are out to fill Yankee Stadium. We believe we have charted a course for ourselves, both on the field and in the front office, that will do both..."
> — Michael Burke, then the president of the Yankees, writing in *Dun's Review*, May 1967. The Yanks finished ninth.

"The next Yankee star is Roger Repoz. There's no question about it."
> — Johnny Johnson, Yankee farm system director, in 1965. Repoz batted .220 that season, four points below his lifetime average.

"The myth is that you put a Yankee uniform on a player and he becomes great."
> — Birdie Tebbetts, former major league player and manager

"You can't let any team awe you. If you do, you'll wind up a horseshit player."

    — Luke Appling, member of the Hall of Fame, on his attitude toward the Yankees during twenty seasons with the Chicago White Sox

"Rooting against the Yankees is like rooting against U.S. Steel."
> — A reporter covering the Dodgers back in 1953, when U.S. Steel was more of a heavy than it is today

"Rooting for the Yankees is like rooting for a yacht."
> — Columnist Jimmy Cannon in 1955

"I won't be active in the day-to-day operations of the club at all. I'll stick to ships."
> — George Steinbrenner after buying the Yankees in 1973

"The only good Yankee is a belly-up Yankee." — Anonymous. DON LORIMER

EPILOGUE

DiMaggio's Unforgettable Record

AUTHORS of Yankee books are required by unwritten law to include a reverent detailing of The Unforgettable Record compiled by Joe DiMaggio, the Immortal Yankee Clipper — IYC for short. So here it is, folks, game by game, the batting record that will never be broken — ten World Series double plays!

1. 1936, Yankees vs. New York Giants, first game, eighth inning. With two runners on and the Yankees trailing by a run, the IYC lined to second baseman Burgess Whitehead, who doubled Red Rolfe off first. End of rally.

2. 1936, fourth game, seventh inning. With runners on first and third and one out, the IYC grounded to shortstop Dick Bartell, who started a double play that ended the inning.

3. 1936, fifth game, fifth inning. With Red Rolfe breaking for second, the IYC swung mightily and struck out. Rolfe was nailed at second base.

4. 1939, Yankees vs. Cincinnati Reds, second game, fifth inning. With one out, Charlie Keller singled, and the IYC grounded to pitcher Bucky Walters for a double play.

5. 1941, Yankees vs. Brooklyn Dodgers, second game, first inning. Rolfe was again the victim as the IYC grounded to Pee Wee Reese at shortstop for a double play.

6. 1941, fifth game, first inning. Poor Rolfe. Once again the IYC fanned as Rolfe broke for the next base. This time he was thrown out at third.

7. 1947, Yankees vs. Dodgers, third game, eighth inning. With the Yankees trailing 9–8, Tommy Henrich walked and Johnny Lindell singled him to second. The IYC grounded to Ed Stanky at second, who tagged Lindell and threw to first for the double play. The rally was killed and the Dodgers won the game.

8. 1947, fifth game, third inning. With one out, Henrich and Lindell walked. Up strode the IYC, who grounded to short for a double play.

9. 1947, fifth game, ninth inning. Could the same two guys get caught in an IYC double play three times in one Series? You bet. Henrich reached first on an error, Lindell was hit by a pitch, and the IYC again grounded to Reese for a double play.

10. 1951, Yankees vs. Giants, second game, first inning. Mickey Mantle and Phil Rizzuto beat out bunts, Gil McDougald singled, and — squelch! — the IYC grounded to Alvin Dark at shortstop for a double play.

There it is, a legendary record that will be talked about as long as the game is played.